Build the Strength Within™

Create the Blueprint for
Your Best Life Yet

DR. DEBORAH CARLIN

SelectBooks, Inc.
New York

This edition published by SelectBooks, Inc.
For information address SelectBooks, Inc., New York, New York.

First Edition

ISBN 978-1-59079-147-9

Library of Congress Cataloging-in-Publication Data
Carlin, Deborah.
 Build the strength within™ : create the blueprint for your best life yet / Dr. Deborah Carlin. --. First Edition.
      pages cm
 Summary: "Author presents her program of a series of self-assessment exercises and plans of action that individuals can follow to create a layout called Blueprint for a Successfully Intentional & Integrated LifeTM. This step-by-step process to map and build a master life plan is intended to help individuals maximize their experience to form the best life possible"-- Provided by publisher.
 ISBN 978-1-59079-147-9 (pbk. : alk. paper)
 1. Self-help techniques. I. Title.
 BF632.C3647 2014
 158--dc23
                        2013045787

Illustrations by Bryan Haynes
Book design and production by Janice Benight

Manufactured in the United States of America

10 9 8 7 6 5 4 3 2 1

Also by Dr. Deborah Carlin

Books
7 Useful Secrets for Discovering the Best Path to Manage Your Stress
Between Magic & Logic: An Educator's Compass for Clarity & Renewal
It's All About Attitude
Pictures From the Heart of a Life
Leadership As a Lifestyle

Audio
The Mind's Eye

Video
The Series 16: The Strength Within

Card Decks
Tools for Building the Strength Within

All of the above are available online at
www.drdebcarlin.com and/or www.amazon.com

Contents

SECTION IV   TAKING IT TO THE NEXT LEVEL   177

Blueprint for a Successfully Intentional & Integrated Life™   176

Introduction to
Build the Strength Within™ Book and Videos

How's it going? Is your life running you, or are you running your life?

My bet is that you are like Atlas, with a whole world of pressure on your shoulders and in your head.

You need to understand how to Build the Strength Within . . .

No matter where we are in life, there are always new opportunities. We need to see them and have the courage to go for them. Whether you want to recharge your business, your relationships, or your health, this is your invitation.

Life is 20 percent mechanics and 80 percent psychology— we all know this.

This event, the one that we call our life, is the opportunity we have to own and influence others to help us succeed on our mission. If you wonder how you can make it happen the way you envision it, allow yourself some confidence, because reaching for new experiences, new guides, and new approaches, are all ways in which you come closer to obtaining what you seek. It is when we sit back and become complacent about what our life is, and what it can be, that we lose our opportunities.

You're joining me for a unique experience, right here in these pages.

Beginning right now, as you open this book and begin to read, you are on a new path of intention. Congratulations. If you will allow me to guide you, you're going to discover that following this book alongside the videos and the audio components is a full-immersion event. I want you to have all the links to our audio and video files. They will enrich your experience. Allow this book and the accompanying materials to impact both the professional and personal relationships in your life by shifting you into a higher and more productive gear and without exhausting you.

How?

I've traveled the globe to study with the best and most insightful business and personal development leaders. I've taken what I have learned from the best, combined it with my formal education and training, and rolled it into what is in my mind and my heart, and I have now put it into a formula that offers you something you've never experienced before. With these materials in your possession, you can continue to work on your life Blueprint, for which a template is provided, and develop your inner strength for the remainder of your beautiful life. The goal is to engage you and get you to tune into other voices that are positive and directive and inspiring. These voices are from the present and also from the deep past. Leonardo da Vinci is an example of this and there are many others. I am not so bold as to think that I have created some brand new invention that is unique; however, I do know that my voice and style of sharing is unique. It is my overt intention here to share the best of my best, and alongside that, the ideas that other great minds have inspired in me. My desire is to inspire you to take time for your *self*-development beyond where you are today. We can use improvement, each one of us . . . always. We are each a work in progress.

Your inner strength is more powerful than you now know—that's a guarantee. I want this experience that you have with me to be phenomenal and to inspire you to be the very best *you*. You're already spectacular; it can only get better. By the way, the fact that you are reading these words is an excellent indication that you'd like to reach for the stars—not just settle for what is currently your situation, but to find a way to become phenomenal in your life.

I know how you feel. Much of what is possible has to do with rewriting your story and reframing your perceptions. This is do-able in ways you've not ever imagined and not in some flakey manner, but in a process that is so genuine you'll wish you'd learned it years ago—really! You'll watch my videos, the ones that gave rise to this book, and at key points you'll listen to the audio for reinforcement of the messaging. There are a total of 16 videos, designed to tune you into what is happening to you on the outside and is impacting you on the inside to stress you out and make you feel weak, tired, and powerless.

But this will happen no more, because you now have the series that provides the *know how* to utilize the tools of vibrance and complete awareness that bring you joy and success. The brightness of the future awaits you.

Each video in *The Series 16* contains the following elements:

Overview and definitions

Explanation of how mindset/attitudes/perception plays a role

Personal stories and theoretical information

Specific exercises to do, skills to develop, and explanations of outcomes to expect

A 3–5 minute closed eye exercise at the end to reinforce the messaging.

There are four segments across *The Series 16*:

The Basics

In this first portion of the series I share with you the very best reasons of why this kind of information is important for each and every one of us, and I also share both the scientific stories as well as the personal ones. I provide you with applications to utilize right from the start.

1. The *you* that awaits your best life yet: how to think about the life you'd like to have

2. Your true inner strength: communication skills with your *self*

3. The magic formula of what to do when and how to do it

Clarity and Application

Once the basics are done, the foundation has been laid and it is time to introduce the element of experience most vibrant for us all.

1. Why I took this journey and how it saved my life

2. When you save your own life, you are available to others

3. Stress and your beautiful body

4. What you put into your mouth and why it matters

5. Movement and alignment and freedom

The Core

In this portion of the series, we enter into the most intimate terrain and expose the thoughts that every human experiences, as I show you how to tap into the solutions to the fears that hold us all back from having our best, richest, most impassioned life.

1. The language of the heart

2. Intimacy with *self* and then others

3. The dance of balance in work

4. Envisioning your fiscal world minus fear

Taking It to the Next Level

This earthly journey is the tangible one, but there is more to contemplate and consider. In these closing segments, you are invited to reach beyond what you now know and consider expansion of your mind, heart, and possibilities.

1. The faith factor

2. Nature, time, and your connection to the earth

3. Life as a cycle intended, not happenstance

4. Stress managed is a life well lived

Additionally, there are 11 self-assessments that you'll take with the plan of action tools that will guide you to clarity and tangible steps to get you on the best path for your best life. In addition, there are exercises, physical, spiritual, psychological, cognitive, and emotional, that are powerful and helpful. I'm so thrilled that you are here. You deserve your best life—grab it! Clarity and application is what I want for you to gain from this series, because if you do, you will absolutely have the strength within you under your influence and at your direction, and you will benefit mightily. I appreciate you being here, so let's get started. It'll be great, and how could it not be.

It's all about you!

BUILD THE STRENGTH WITHIN™

Tune into what is happening to you on the outside and impacting you on the inside to make you feel weak, tired, and powerless. With *The Series 16* videos and book for *Build the Strength Within™* you now have a full-life program of exercises and tools to turn this around, allowing you to make your plan to find joy and success.

Enrich your life by creating the blueprint for your best life yet.

Dear friend in search of the best life yet,

Let's cut to the chase on this one. None of us have time to waste, it is a limited commodity and before we know it time is up, expired, done, and we need to have used our life time well if we want for our death to be less agonizing.

Many people grow up and think that their life was somehow unique. The only portion of our experience that is unique is that it is ours. Reality is that all humans share the dynamics of this journey and it is filled with joy, sorrow, agony, ecstasy . . . a good life is the full ride. Whatever our story is about, it is a matter of reality based upon perceptions . . . and we can work with that . . . and we can rewrite it . . . every bit of it . . . trust that notion, it will serve you well . . . and within your exposure to me and to these materials, you'll learn how.

There are many blessing to be found within . . . both these pages and also you.

This, my friends, is what my parents raised me on.

For real,
Deb

Section I
THE BASICS

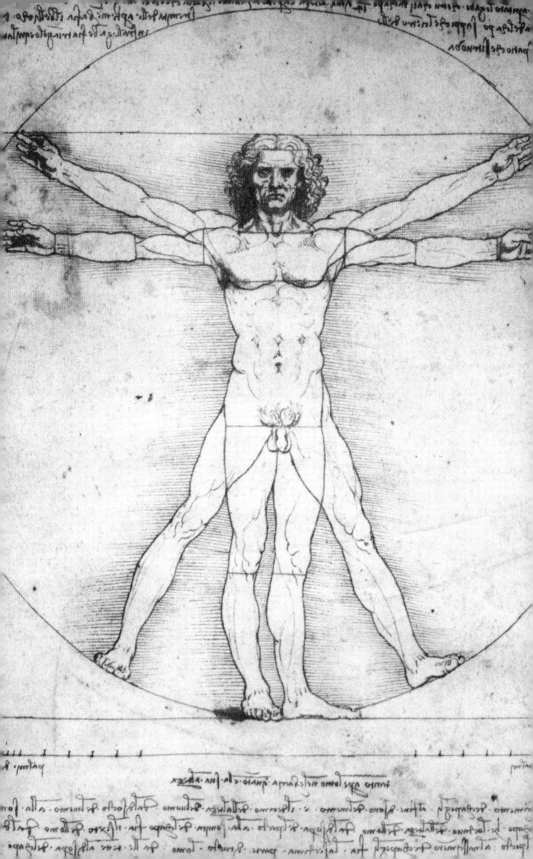

Prelude

LEONARDO DI SER PIERO DA VINCI

His life was not one of luxury or ease. He was hard working and diligent. He is well known for his expressiveness in the private writings he entered in his notebooks on a daily basis. His life and his works and his wonderful notebooks can serve as an inspiration for us all.

The man we know as Leonardo da Vinci was born in Florence, Italy on April 15, 1452, and died on May 2, 1519, in Amboise, France. He is the genius who brought us the Mona Lisa, The Last Supper, and Vitruvian Man.

Leonardo da Vinci conceptualized the helicopter, the tank, solar power, the calculator, and the double hull. His boundless imagination was fueled by his curiosity and his desire to write about and illustrate his musings. All that he dreamt of producing was not feasible in the era of his life, but his notebooks and creations have inspired us for centuries and will continue to do so.

In 1502 he sketched a design for a bridge that he intended for the Turkish Sultan Bajazet II. The project was declined because the sultan could not embrace the revolutionary pressed-bow engineering and 720 foot span, claiming it was simply "too fantastic." That was more than 400 years ago. However, in the late 1990s, his sketches ignited the imagination of an artist who brought the vision to fruition. In 2001 Queen Sonja of Norway dedicated Vebjorn Sand's bridge, the first civil engineering project based on a Leonardo da Vinci design to be constructed. This pedestrian footbridge linking Norway and Sweden is named Leonardo's Bridge.

Inspiration lives inside of each one of us . . . it is strengthened or diminished by those we associate with, as well as what it is we say to ourselves. History teaches us that our genius is indomitable. Let's tap it!

Blueprint for a Successfully Intentional & Integrated Life

Y ou can pick up a set of blueprints for anything, anything that you want to build. We primarily turn to blueprints for putting together a house, one to be planned out carefully by a qualified architect, and perhaps involving an engineer. We seek out people who can help us when we have a big and unfamiliar project, one unfamiliar to us and in need of special expertise.

Typically, if a project seems pretty simple, we just proceed with the confidence that we can get it done. If it is a project that comes with a booklet, we look at the instruction sheet. And even then, we often proceed with a certain confidence, maybe arrogance, that we don't really need that instruction guide, we can just look at the picture and put it all together, make it happen.

Sound familiar?

And sometimes it actually all works out . . . and sometimes, it just doesn't.

When it comes to our life, we very often fly by the seat of our pants and assume things will unfold as society, or our family, tells us it will. We look at a picture of life and we anticipate. We allow life to just happen. We put one foot in front of the other and we expect matriculation, on every front. Sometimes we are lucky and sometimes we are not. I've never really been 100 percent certain about what exactly luck is, my hunch is that it is a lure to test if we are paying attention.

There is a problem with living life with the anticipation *it will all just work out*. People, from childhood on, expect to be passed from one grade to the next—as though there is an entitlement from just simply being present. That breeds false confidence. There is another expectation during adolescence that because there is a social event like a prom or a party or a dance or a concert, everyone will be invited, invited to attend, to be part of the party . . . and that leads to expectations and disappointment when it doesn't just happen. College and first jobs are often places where a spouse is found and so the pressure is on. Alongside, there is expectation and also demand. Timing alone is not what makes for great life choices. However, the combination of timing with readiness and awareness does.

People get married every day as the result of an expectation—expectation from within, from friends, from family, from society—children get conceived for similar reasons. Life without planning that makes good sense across all dimensions is a life of happenstance. Sometimes it appears as if it actually works and other times, it doesn't come even close. All you need to do is look at national statistics and the reality presents itself that these statements have merit. Our culture knows all too well the prevalence of adultery, marital separation, divorce, unwanted pregnancy, child abuse, financial collapse, etcetera, etcetera, etcetera.

Move along further and note that marriages are expected to be happy and monogamous. This leads to expectations and frequent disappointment, too. Children are brought into the world and the expectation is that they will be normal and excel and be productive and fold into the family routines, but without a solid knowing, awareness, structure, plan, and follow through, disappointment and dysfunction emerge. And then even with the best of intentions, things happen . . . all sorts of things. How do you navigate?

Jobs are expected to be fabulous and with an upward mobility in financial reward and in status and responsibility. The life path toward retirement is supposed to land us all in the Golden Years . . . but you won't often hear seniors bragging about how golden their senior experience feels. What is the plan for your senior experience? Will you be surprised to be alone in your own home or in a nursing home? What's your intention?

Do you live your life with forethought and intention?

State here what your evidence is for either.

Here's my question for you: how many of these components of our life story have a plan, a blueprint—something that places us on an intentional track and prompts us to be accountable and proactive?

What does each decade of your life look like for you?

Go back in time. Review and write what the plan was then and whose it was . . .

Until you were 10 years old

Until you were 20

During your 20s

During your 30s

Either continue to look back or look ahead and ask yourself what it will look like, what the plan is, whose plan it is:

During your 40s

During your 50s

During your 60s

During your 70s

During your 80s

During your 90s

What Is Your Blueprint . . .

The big question for you is:

What are you going to do to make this happen?

Does your life and the quality of this one-life experience matter to you?

Do you believe you have influence over your life? Or does it just happen to you?

Are you a bystander or an active and influencing participant?

Are you a dreamer who dreams and acts upon making dreams come true?

Do you just dream to pretend and let the dreams float by like clouds in the sky?

Are you satisfied with the style with which you are living your life?

Are you willing to be a creative, vibrant, and smart architect and shape the life you crave?

What are you willing to do in order to make it happen?

As shared earlier, your Intentional Life Blueprint needs to be a multidimensional document that is representative of all the things that impact the life experience and the way we deal with it at each important juncture. In this book and the creation of your Blueprint that coincides with it, the focus is on exposing you to 11 dimensions of self-assessment that guide you to have clarity about your *self*. Granted, there are many more we can add but this is a solid platform for beginning the work.

Thus far, you've answered questions on the over-arching themes. Now is the time to dive into each of the components. We'll return to what you've already done as we put the Blueprint together as we move through the material.

Working through each of the following will help you build your Blueprint. Let's get started in conjunction with the material we cover here as well as your review of the videos and materials over time. It is important to make note that just as is the case of having an organizational strategic plan, a **Blueprint for a Successfully Intentional and Integrated Life**™ is a fluid creation that needs attention and updating with consistency and intention. It is also important to note that we will move through the assessments more than once—the re-visits are necessary and helpful.

The following are the assessments that will be covered in this book. They include tools called "Plans Of Action" to be used to build your

Blueprint for a Successfully Intentional & Integrated Life™

The Brain Power
Self-Determination & Resolution
Freedom of Movement
Work Life Integration
Mind & Body Integration

Multidimensional Health Locus of Control
Speed of Trust
Your Fiscal Comfort Zone Today
The Faith Factor
Expectations of Success
Movement & Desire

Reading the works of great minds who have thought about and studied the human experience can be helpful and very illuminating. We will begin here with Erik Erikson as our guide to help us understand our life experience thus far, and this will give us contemplative material about what to consider now in order to plan for a bright, emotionally successful future.

If you find yourself resisting the idea of taking a look in your rearview mirror, bear with me. I understand. My intention for you is to have you develop an ever more productive and keen awareness of you as a person, of who you are, and about the path that you have landed on and are on today. I have a desire for you to look at your life with compassion for every single event that has taken place for you.

This is important. ——

UNDERSTANDING ERIKSON
1902–1994

Erik Erikson is a world famous psychologist who wrote many volumes about the development of the human being. He was a theorist who described the various stages in the life cycle in terms of social psychology.

Infancy	Trust vs. mistrust
2nd year	Autonomy vs. shame and doubt
3rd–5th year	Initiative vs. guilt
6th–12th year	Industry vs. inferiority
Adolescence	Identity vs. role confusion
Adulthood	Intimacy vs. isolation
Middle adulthood	Generativity vs. stagnation
Late adulthood	Integrity vs. despair

Each stage is based upon our interactions with the world, including how we interpret the events of our daily living, what we do in our mind with our perceptions—and how we write our life experience, our life story. Where do you want to land?

The stages that Erikson mapped out are across a range and he establishes extreme options on either end. There are, of course, many areas in between the extreme ends. These stages are psychological and social, as well as emotional. When you stop to contemplate what he communicated, it is clear that he was attempting to encourage us to find a way to end up with a life experience that begins with trust and ends with integrity.

Infants come to know the world through the experiences they have with their caregivers. If your basic physiological needs are met, as well as your social and emotional needs, you come to know the world as a pretty nifty place to be, one where people love you and take good and nurturing care of you. You don't want for anything, at least not for very long. The attended baby learns to trust that their needs are important to others and will be taken care of thoughtfully. Trust evolves.

A child who lives in an atmosphere where these needs either cannot be met, or simply are not met, suffers greatly. They suffer physically, and they also suffer psychologically. Life is impossible without the care of others, particularly when you are a helpless infant. These concepts are more than intangible psychological theories; there is an observable impact on us at both extremes across each one of our life stages.

When we come to the ending chapters in this book of our life, Erikson sees that we either feel positive or negative about the way we are invested in our mind and heart and our activities. Understandably, we either feel a sense of pride and integrity, or else have a feeling of hopelessness about not having more opportunities to create the life we realize we have wanted all along.

His theory of human development is taught to students in every general psychology course and people entering into a broad range of professions receive this knowledge—such as teachers, nurses, and medical students—who all get a taste of this perspective. I have studied his work from the time I was in college, by reading his original works during graduate school, and teaching his theory for more than two decades in university settings, where the topic was human development. I think Erikson is sensible and offers us a way to better understand our own self and as well as others.

I invite you to read the following more in-depth review that puts into perspective why it is helpful to consider the value each life stage can offer. Be compassionate about your awareness and tolerance. You are simply tuning into perception. It gives us a handle to implement change—a change that is productive.

As you read what follows here, indicate on each continuum where it is you think and feel you have landed in your development. Please note that the time frames are general, not rigid.

1. Infancy: the first year
Trust vs. Mistrust
There is no denying that infancy is a time of complete dependence for the infant; they are at the mercy of their care provider. When babies cry, they have a need of some sort. The manner in which their needs are

handled teaches them that the world is either a safe place where they can trust others or they learn that it is not, and they become fearful.

It makes sense that if the mom or dad hears a baby cry out and comes to offer comfort and affection to relieve the baby's angst, a healthy bond is formed. If there is either no parental reaction or an unpleasant one, fear and anxiety would be the infant's experience.

Although it is just a theory, Erikson's assumption is based upon the idea that we learn about the world and our relation to others from the very beginning of our life experience, and our initial caregivers are the teachers. Patterns in relationships then set in early and accompany us through our life.

The question for you is: how trusting are you? Can you envision why you are where you have landed on the continuum?

Trust ←++++++++++++++++++++++++++→ **Mistrust**

2. Toddlerhood: the second year
Autonomy vs. Shame

Emerging from infancy, the baby begins to explore the world with new mobility and curiosity. There are phases of competency for crawling and toddling and walking; each is met with an inner sense of satisfaction or failure. Each has an impact upon self-image and self-esteem and the ability to further encourage autonomy.

As a toddler meets with success at crawling, getting up, and toddling she or he walks and eventually begins to run. Each stumble is a slight setback that presents a choice of perseverance or defeat. This concept extends across each of the major developmental challenges that take place during this year, including toilet training and the introduction of the concept of our needing to have boundaries. Boundaries are the social perimeters we come to learn about that establish appropriate social behaviors.

The child's audience offers feedback about his or her attempts to achieve whatever the task is. Positive encouragement leads to pride and motivates the drive for autonomy. Criticism is demeaning and creates a sense of shame.

The invitation for you here is to think about how you got to be where you are in your life with respect to these concepts. It is not about blaming anyone; it is about attempting to gain a deeper sense of appreciation for who you are and the depth of your inner sense of positive self.

Autonomy ◄┼┼┼┼┼┼┼┼┼┼┼┼┼┼┼► Shame

3. Early childhood: 3 to 5 years old
Initiative vs. Guilt

As each stage builds upon the previous one, the child becomes increasingly more explorative and interactive with his or her environment. It is through social interactions and the continuation of testing their skills that the sense of accomplishment is experienced at a deeper level, both emotionally and cognitively. The concept of self-esteem is important and every human being craves a positive sense of who they are and what they can accomplish. With positive outcomes for what is attempted, there is a positive reinforcement for taking initiative and continuing developmental explorations. When there is an unsuccessful outcome to initiatives taken, especially if there is an audience that is punitive, there is a feeling of guilt—a remorse or shame for not being good enough.

People often make the mistake of underestimating what children think and feel. Doing so is a mistake. Our identity is formed in our early years and it is based upon the exposure we have to the world we are developing within.

The question for you to ask yourself and to be reflective about concerns the perspective you have about taking initiative. Consider whether you enjoy it or shrink from it because of frustration and feelings of guilt that come from childhood experience.

Initiative ◄┼┼┼┼┼┼┼┼┼┼┼┼┼┼┼► Guilt

4. Elementary school age: 6 to 12 years old
Industry vs. Inferiority

The experiences that take place during the elementary school years leave a lasting impression, which the child is now mature enough to process information in additionally complex ways. The concept of competition is alive and real and plays an important role in the social atmosphere. Children begin to establish a sense of where they fit in a social order and their awareness offers them an opportunity to either feel industrious and competent or inferior and diminished.

It is important to note that this is the developmental time of puberty. Children's bodies become less familiar and more mysterious to them with rapidly changing developments that can happen within the course of a day or overnight. Hair grows in odd places, a voice cracks while a boy is speaking, the sweat glands emit an odor that causes embarrassment, and there are sexual developments that are a challenge to manage. The body perplexes the mind and the emotions are confused.

The ability to be industrious has many implications that extend from the need for cognitive abilities to having physical and emotional skills. The experience of feeling inferior affects a wide range of dimensions within a person. The negative feelings established at this time can be life-long unless there is some interruption in the development that changes the reality of the outcomes the child is able to produce.

The work of the Build the Strength Within program offers an opportunity to find the pathway towards industrious competency by having the belief that it is present in every person. The task for you at this point is to reflect upon how much success you had in your early life and ask how it has impacted your adulthood.

Industry ◄┼┼┼┼┼┼┼┼┼┼┼┼┼┼┼► **Inferiority**

5. Adolescence: 12 to 19 years old
Identity vs. Role Confusion

For many years, adolescent development was my favorite class to teach at the university. Working with college students who held an initial belief that they were adults fascinated me. At an opening class, I would ask them to raise their hands if they thought of themselves as children, adolescents, or adults. The majority thought they were adults.

Their perceptions shifted when the questions continued about who paid their bills, purchased their automobiles, and bought their clothing. It was additionally revealing when the questions were about their life choices and career pursuits.

Throughout childhood many games are played and children try on various roles to discover what feels like a good fit. During adolescence, the child is now more diligent about experimenting with their identity and how they want to look and act, who they want be associated with, and how they want to invest their energy towards some lifestyle goal. They are also under pressure from others to investigate life paths and academic courses to create the correct path for their future.

High school and college are turbulent times as the experimentation takes place, and they meet with some success as well as failures. Simultaneously, they go through additional physiological changes during this time of post puberty when they adapt to a more adult version of their body. In the later teenage years, kids look like adults but they are still discovering who they are and who it is they want to become. Society treats them more like adults, but they have not yet arrived.

It seems that some people never emerge to an understanding about who they are and what their role is, and they remain life-long adolescents. Where are you with respect to this? Have you figured it out?

Identity ◄┼┼┼┼┼┼┼┼┼┼┼┼┼┼┼► **Role Confusion**

6. Young adulthood
Intimacy vs. Isolation

The pressure is on to become a grown-up person and further the family lineage and the species. After high school and college, there is a cultural anticipation of selecting a mate, building a home together, and creating a family. These steps imply a capacity for intimacy with another on every level.

However, there are challenges. Depending on how the developmental process has gone thus far, some people find it easier to isolate than to risk the vulnerability of intimacy. The problem is that life is not a fully rich experience without the experience of the depth intimate relationships—the genuine bearing of the soul to another.

These are the years of fertility when it is most natural to mate and reproduce. Regardless of the options that technology and society has introduced, these ideas of the stages of human development, based on the theories of a man who lived in a different era, continue to make psychological sense as we seek to better understand how to have a full and rich life.

Where are you on the continuum?

Intimacy ◄┼┼┼┼┼┼┼┼┼┼┼┼┼┼┼► **Isolation**

7. Middle Adulthood:

Generativity vs. Stagnation

It is important to recognize that with each developmental stage shown here, there are physical realities that impact our choices and abilities to explore life options. Although there is a longer time period in this stage, there is a certain shift that comes with a mature appreciation of aging. Presumably the mate is selected, the children are present, and the family is functioning. The time has arrived to focus on taking care of the people you have created.

Career and work become a dominant focus, no matter what is chosen—whether it occurs at home or out in the workplace. By the time a person reaches this phase in their life, the individual feels a certain authority because of decades of experience. There is now time to either share wisdom or selfishly believe there is not any reason to contribute to society or continue to grow for the betterment of the self and the culture.

Some people describe this period of their life as the most vibrant because they are old enough to have a realization of their wisdom and are still young enough to be able to explore how best to apply it. The question for you is, depending upon your age, where are you and where do you want to be in relation to this continuum?

Generativity ◄┼┼┼┼┼┼┼┼┼┼┼┼┼┼► **Stagnation**

8. Late Adulthood

Integrity vs. Despair

As we age, there is an awareness of how much time is left in relation to how much time has been spent. No matter which decade we are in at this stage, there is less time ahead than there is behind, so it is natural to look back and ask about the choices made and options taken. There is a certain element of despair about wanting to do some parts over and produce different outcomes.

The goal for *Build the Strength Within* is to raise the awareness of every person and to inspire a reach for a life plan that includes the anticipation of this stage and the desire for it to be one filled with integrity and very little despair. Despair is about profound regret. Regret robs a person of the happiness she or he might have the capacity for.

It is when there is a plan of action and a life that is intentional that a person has an opportunity for feelings of satisfaction for what was attempted and hopefully accomplished in this life experience. Spending time with the elderly is very educational if you allow it to be. People who have reached their eight and ninth decades of life with integrity can teach the younger how to navigate a life for fulfillment.

Those who are dying have lessons to share as well. To die with despair is heartbreaking for anyone to experience and also to witness. The question for you here is: what do you want in your final chapters? None of us gets out of here alive; we need to plan for our exit.

Integrity ◄—┼—┼—┼—┼—┼—┼—┼—┼—┼—┼—┼—┼—► **Despair**

The information from Erikson invites you to take another look at your own life. Stop and ask yourself where you see yourself in each stage. Give yourself time to think about how you have dealt with your circumstances. As you do this, please bear in mind that it is not ever too late to rewrite your life story, to recover from hurt or even from trauma. The path towards your best life yet begins with a desire for it and continues with a determination to be aware—aware of your own self and aware of the ways in which you have, thus far, experienced and interpreted this life experience. You'll be invited to work on your Blueprint at key points in this book.

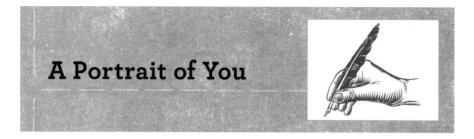

A Portrait of You

Take some time, right now . . . for you. You've just been exposed to some thought-provoking ideas. Now it is time to draw. Or sketch. Don't worry about artistic quality. Just let your hand and your mind work together.

As author Michael Gelb shares with us in his many writings inspired by the notebooks of Leonardo da Vinci, there is great benefit to having a journal, a notebook in which you find time to write and to sketch. Leonardo wrote "Feathers shall raise men even as they do birds, toward heaven; that is by letters written with their quills." Inspired, indeed—let it be contagious.

Draw a portrait of who you are . . . don't over think this . . . just draw who you are, what you are. I will share information with you later that you will find helpful in understanding what you create in these sketches.

SELF-ASSESSMENT
Brain Power

The way that we use our mind is something we take for granted, repeatedly. We are routinely doing what we do to the point that we don't even realize the power and magnitude of it. When people become impaired however, from a stroke or some form of dementia, they note how compartments of the brain contribute to what they are able to do—or not. In our healthy years, there are things we can observe, learn about, and utilize to strengthen the power of our mind, but first we must get acquainted.

What is it about the mind that is so fascinating?

Why do we get afraid of our own thoughts . . . and the thoughts of others?

Do you understand your mind as deeply as you think you could?

The opening question for you here is: how would an understanding of the way that your brain, and the brain of others, operates help you to be more effective? Think carefully, reply to the questions.

Answer honestly. If you don't, then this is just a silly game that is a waste of time, especially yours.

1 = not at all   9 = all the way

1. I have an extremely flexible mind.

    1   2   3   4   5   6   7   8   9

2. I understand the structure of my mind and how best I file information for later recall.

    1   2   3   4   5   6   7   8   9

3. I am completely aware of how I take in information most effectively.

    1   2   3   4   5   6   7   8   9

4. I am a master communicator because I understand how others need to hear me.

    1   2   3   4   5   6   7   8   9

5. I can learn very well in any format, any environment.

    1   2   3   4   5   6   7   8   9

6. I am well acquainted with visual learning techniques.

    1   2   3   4   5   6   7   8   9

7. I am well acquainted with auditory learning techniques.

    1   2   3   4   5   6   7   8   9

8. I am well acquainted with kinesthetic learning techniques.

    1   2   3   4   5   6   7   8   9

9. I know my learning style and easily assess others' learning styles.

    1   2   3   4   5   6   7   8   9

PLAN OF ACTION TOOL
Think Like da Vinci

Well-known author Michael Gelb has what I consider to be a fabulous mind and personality. He is impressively curious about how best to live this life productively and fully engaged. He has studied Leonardo da Vinci extensively and has written about the man and his incredible habits and ideas in his international best seller *How to Think Like Leonardo da Vinci: Seven Steps to Genius Every Day*. We have much to learn from both of them.

One of the habits Michael Gelb encourages is to write, sketch, doodle, and draw all day and every day. This is what Leonardo did. He always had a notebook of some sort in hand and he never missed recording a thought. Think now for a moment about all the times you had a good idea but had so many interruptions between the time of insight to writing it, that it simply evaporated. Stop that now. Capture your great ideas.

This book provides plenty of open space for you to write, sketch, and draw . . . so start now.

What follows is a link you will absolutely love. It is a presentation by Gelb where he explains what he found when he immersed himself into Leonardo. Fascinating.

One of his essential findings is the observation of what are entitled:

Seven da Vincian Principles

Seven Steps to Genius Every Day: How to Think Like Leonardo da Vinci

CURIOSITA
Approaching life with insatiable curiosity and an unrelenting quest for continuous learning

DIMOSTRAZIONE
Committing to test knowledge through experience, persistence, and a willingness to learn from mistakes

SENSAZIONE
Continually refining the senses, especially sight, as the means to enliven experience

SFUMATO
Embracing ambiguity, paradox, and uncertainty

ARTE/SCIENZA
Balancing science and art, logic, and imagination: "whole-brain thinking"

CORPORALITA
Cultivating grace, ambidexterity, fitness, and poise

CONNESSIONE
Recognizing and appreciating the interconnectedness of all things: "systems thinking"

The following website can guide you even deeper.
http://michaelgelb.com/

PLAN OF ACTION TOOL
Luminosify

The Internet is a great invention; some smart person had a vision and saw it through to fruition, and many hands and brains joined in to make it is what we know it to be today. Utilizing Google.com is amazing. Enter in brain games, brain fun, brain growth, brain exercises, and a world opens with invitations for where to invest your attention. Lumosity is one of my favorite sites at www.lumosity.com and they even define themselves for us.

Lumosify (v)
To sharpen your memory, focus your attention, and brighten your future

Memory

Problem Solving

Attention

Speed

Flexibility

This group extends beyond games, but they do indeed make stretching your brain power fun. You can join their e-list and get tuned into updates and offers daily to make this part of your action plan for your Blueprint.

It's hard to imagine that until only a few short decades ago, scientists believed that the human brain was born with its ultimate capacity and death of brain cells set in after the first breath. Intelligence was thought to be fixed and limited. Of course, there were those who disagreed, but the trend was to follow this conventional myth—this happens and people get locked into it. Thankfully, however, it is clear that the brain is nearly boundless and has the phenomenal ability to regenerate itself and take over areas where there is damage. There is a fascinating concept called plasticity that describes this idea in depth.

Think about it. Consider all the ways in which most people are not trained to think of their brain as something they need to get hold of in order to seriously direct the energies of their mind. In fact, stop and think about what happens when someone buys a puppy. The person spends spend time, energy, effort, money, and heart and soul training a puppy to understand that the outside world is their bathroom, not the interior floors of their home. Right? And most people spend a similar amount of time training their puppy to walk on a leash so they are not dragged about. In some respects, our mind is like that puppy; it needs to be directed, trained, and often put on a leash to control where it goes.

The question here is, do you have a leash for your mind? Do you actively direct where your thoughts go or do you just get dragged along like an innocent bystander?

What's inside your skull is yours to direct, influence, control, nourish, exercise, and rest . . .

How would you like to begin doing that?

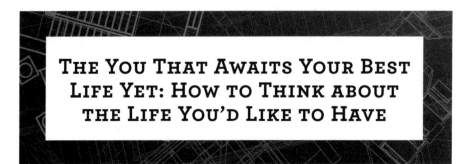

THE YOU THAT AWAITS YOUR BEST LIFE YET: HOW TO THINK ABOUT THE LIFE YOU'D LIKE TO HAVE

I grew up thinking how fabulous it would be to be all grown up. I envisioned a life where no one could boss me around because I was just a little kid or a teenager. To be an adult meant to be free and doing what I wanted, whenever I wanted. It would be great! What a surprise to arrive at my 20s and 30s and beyond and realize that there is no such life; we are all accountable to lots of people all through our lifetime, and really, for *ever*, regardless of what age we are. The ideas I had about independence were some sort of twisted version of how it would all happen without any hassle, but in truth, there is no such way. We are all here to be interdependent and reliant upon one another for all sorts of things, from helping each other with simple tasks, and forming relationships of friendships, deep love, and liking, to requiring others for professional services and guidance for one thing or another. We also need to acquiesce to our community's authority of the law and rules—even the simple ones like adhering to the rules to stay off the playing field at the ball park to make certain everyone is safe. *Every* one of us needs lots of other people in order for our lives to work. Life means cooperation.

The problem is that people can really drive you nuts, can't they? I'm a psychologist and I always think I should understand everything about everyone, but the fact is that some people really tic me off and others just cause me to roll my eyes. Some people make me screaming mad, I mean really mad, even if it is just a situation on the telephone when I find myself caught in one of those obnoxious phone messaging systems when what I really need is to reach a live human being—or when I finally do reach a live person but they don't speak my language. We've all been there. We've all had fits and had our guts twisted in a knot and felt sick over some sort of frustrating situation.

And then there is also the element of surprise in life. There are things that happen that you didn't anticipate, like illness, financial crisis, employment changes, death of a loved one, natural disasters, going to war, a missing pet. I could go on, but I don't want to become depressing here; things just happen in this life and we are sometimes on the receiving end of difficult times. Period.

I've had a whole lot of advantages in my life, and I am well aware that I have a lot to be grateful for. I was born into a terrific, healthy, privileged, American family with strong values and all sorts of opportunities. However, growing up in the middle of that was my reality, I didn't have a perspective that I was somehow fortunate. I heard that I was lucky and I was frequently told that I was, but I didn't get it because the life we live is what we know, and somehow we all want something else or something different.

For example, I remember vividly when I was told to finish my supper, even when it was something I absolutely hated, because "there are children starving in India and China." But it fell on deaf ears and my only response was—and I mean this seriously—"Okay, then let's box it up and send it to *them*." That, by the way, is the wrong comeback to your mom and dad even if you're sincere, and this behavior that causes extreme stress is just plain stupid. The point is that I had no idea about the blessings I was sitting in the middle of, but what I did know was that I had dreams, all sorts of day dreams, that began when I was very little and they changed and shifted and developed just as I did.

My life dreams were about a bigger house that would be my own house and it'd be exactly how I wanted it. I'd have all sorts of people there to pick up after me and to do the things I didn't ever want to have to do again. I'd have my own beach, horses, dogs, a handsome prince charming, and fabulous children of my own. I'd also have a life of fun and travel and helping people and a loving family and would be healthy and strong while enjoying the holidays and picnics and parties and lots of wonderful friends who were always good and very loyal. The dreams also included having something that I would do that was important and would make me rich, and my dreams also included my never having any worries.

I envisioned this and dreamed about it but had no clue about how to achieve it. Quite frankly, most people don't, and so they go down a particular path in life that *seems* like the right thing to do. And then they wonder how they land where they find themselves and get frustrated about what the heck happened. We all get stuck, and when we get stuck in the day-to-day dealings of tasks and facing hassles, we stop dreaming with any real clarity or positive intention. All too frequently we, *people everywhere*, experience frustration about not having what we want. It seems unfair and wrong and like somehow we missed the boat or got cheated. It's awful. It is an awful thought to have and it is really an awful perspective to adopt because it leads into having an attitude that is completely counterproductive to getting what you want out of this life.

So if all of that is true, even to only a small degree, how do you get the life that you want? What if you're already stuck in some sickening situation you want out of? Or what if you're just adrift and not yet certain of what you really want? Or maybe you're just tired and can't even think of how to pull it together to make anything happen.

I want to share a bit of something with you that I have learned, and I mean mightily so: *You have all sorts of power within you to make happen whatever life you seriously desire.* I am not kidding. You don't have to believe it, but you're going to be happier if you allow yourself to believe it. I guarantee this is true.

I've worked with all sorts of people in my personal life and in my career and I see components of myself in just about everyone I deal with, even when I don't like what I am seeing; there are just simply parts of the human spirit that are consistent across all of us. When I work with someone who is in some form of trouble, and I hear the person list off the long litany of reasons about why their life is stinky—because of their family, because of their friends, because of their spouse, because of their kids, because of their health, because of their boss, because of the government—it all comes down to looking outside for answers instead of looking into the mirror. The mirror is the toughest place I will ever send a human being. More on that later, but believe me, now, it is a very rough place to spend time.

The secret, and I really do mean that it is a big, huge, fat secret, is that your mind is what controls your world and directs the course of events in your life. If you see and think about drama that is creepy and ugly, you will be there because you *are* there. Sounds weird, right? Think about it. You can get yourself into a completely rotten frame of mind if you allow it. You've done it before. You know you have. And you can also get yourself happy and loose and lively because of what and how you think, and you have done that before too. The trick is to become more aware of this and also more intentional.

Guess what the really groovy news is about all of this? *You can change it all around and immediately . . . and I mean like right this very second!* And by change I mean that you can increase your level of awareness and experience control within yourself that alters your life experience in an ongoing manner. I am going to give you an exercise right now and have you simply participate. And it is the beginning of what you are going to start doing, and it is going to change your life and rock your world and make your dreams unfold and come into being. All you have to do is get on board and cooperate . . . and believe.

Your Self Talk Script

I want you to sit down or lie down and get really comfy, and relax. Wander into your mind and ignite the dreams that are waiting for you to kindle them—they are dreams from a time when you allowed your mind to drift and to see the potential of your life . . . you remember what they were . . . you had them as a child, you made them vivid as a teen . . . you craved them when you were in your 20s and you can recall them right now . . . just breathe . . . rejuvenate the ideas of how you want your life to be spent, who you want to be in all your greatest glory, who you want beside you to enjoy every moment of it . . . and what you want to feel at the end of each day as you lie down and drift off into your night of slumber and rest. Dream now, relax and float into the mind that is yours . . . allow your dreams to envelop you and allow yourself to embrace them again . . . see them . . . feel them, rich and deep and real . . . do this now and hold the feeling and hold the seeing of it . . . all of it . . . it is yours, and since it is yours, you have it . . . you need to realize every aspect of It, and you can . . . you can . . . you can . . . . . . tell yourself that you can . . . anything is possible . . .

Stay here and relax and breathe and enjoy what you unearth . . .

To view the video: www.drdebcarlin.com

Your TRUE Inner Strength:
Communication Skills
with your SELF

I invited you to relax and enjoy your experience of dreaming about your life and what you really desire deep inside of yourself for this life experience. Did you make note of the things that got in the way, the many things you ended up thinking about and saying to yourself, the things that make you a skeptic and a disbeliever about what you can get out of this life? Or just simply things that are distracters—like I wonder what time it is, did I remember to buy coffee at the grocery? It's important to pay attention to what your mind does when you give it an assignment, because too often we allow it to drift and do not attend to where it goes. It's almost like we are led around by our mind instead of our leading where our mind travels. It sounds kind of silly when you say that out loud, but think about that. I've thought about it a whole lot and have then looked to learn more about that line of thinking and about thinking about thinking.

We each have our own style and ways of wanting to know more about a given topic. For me, I most often turn to the written word to learn about things. There are some wonderful authors in the world. I love to read, and have found great benefit from reading, especially everything that people like Wayne Dyer, Tony Robbins, Maya Angelou, and Stephen Covey have written. There are many more; these are just some of my favorites.

As a professional, I have a library full of books written by great authors who are often scientists who explain their research and go deep into their methodology and statistical analysis. I find it fascinating. Mostly, I love gathering information and examining it for credibility—I want to discover truths. I crave learning what is helpful both for me and for people in general. My belief is that if it is helpful for one person, it can be for many, and if many people are helped, the world is simply a better place to live in.

One of the topics I started thinking about as a child was "self talk." My mother, God bless her soul, was a truly wise woman. She would talk to me about talking to myself. She encouraged it. She often did this as a means to encourage me to be a good little girl in anticipation of Santa and the promise of the great gifts he was capable of bringing each December if you had been good. It was very effective. She'd remind me that it was easy to think good thoughts and then do good deeds, but you had to start with the right good thoughts. I thought she was kind of funny sometimes because of these kind of odd conversations we'd have, but when I paid even a little bit of attention to her direction, I realized how correct and intuitive she was about human nature.

As the years went on, I began working with patients. Initially I worked with people who had cardiovascular disease, including heart attacks, high blood pressures, strokes, and angina. I began talking to them about their thinking and their self-talk. I found some very interesting patterns, and when I reviewed the materials in my library, I found strong and very compelling evidence that what we say to our *self* has a direct influence on what happens to our body, to our own physiology, and also leads to the events in our life.

If you read books like Dean Ornish's *Open Your Heart Program,* Herbert Benson's *Relaxation Response,* or *The Language of the Heart* by James Lynch, you'll find fascinating accounts of just how powerful your mind is over your body and the way it functions. You'll come to see clearly that you have enormous influence over your physiology. It's pretty cool stuff. I will share more about the details of all of this later.

Dean Ornish explains that, from his research, he consistently finds that people can change their diet and exercise program to recover from cardiovascular events, but the one thing that makes the difference between life and death is the ability to relax the mind. He has done great work, and in his research programs he spends intensive time with his patients, teaching them and guiding them in groups about the foods they eat and about the exercises to participate in. He also works to have them learn relaxations and meditations. He had one man, in particular, who was very compliant with everything except the meditations and relaxations.

When the group would begin these relaxation exercises, the man would instead go for a run or hard workout of some sort. He just didn't participate, for whatever his reasoning was. Unfortunately, it became clear that his inner chatter was very counterproductive and negative given his continual anger and despair. He was tough on himself and he had thinking patterns that were uncontrolled in destructive ways, and he was the one patient during Dr. Ornish's initial research who died. He died of the very things that he was trying to recover from during his heart disease. The emotional autopsy made it pretty clear that had he been able to relax the mind, there would've been excellent, healthy, benefits for his body.

So what happens to make the effect of our mind on our body so powerful?

The most powerful reality is that our body does what our mind directs, and so when we are laughing and enjoying an experience, our body is releasing chemicals from our brain into our system that relax our body and make us feel great. Laughter is actually a highly complex process; it involves complicated brain activities leading to a positive effect on our overall health. In the early 1970s Norman Cousins, who was the long-time editor of the *Saturday Review*, suggested the idea that humor and the associated laughter can benefit a person's health. His ground-breaking work, as a layperson diagnosed with an autoimmune disease, documented his use of laughter in treating himself—with medical approval and oversight—right into remission. He published his personal research results in the *New England Journal of Medicine* and is considered one of the original architects of mind-body medicine. His books, *Anatomy of an Illness*, *The Healing Heart*, and *Head First* are excellent resources of great information.

Cousins' pioneering work began with his frustrations about how people treat you when you are sick, especially while you're in the hospital. In fact, his inspiration was his agony, which was a direct result of his hospital stay. Frustrated by the depressing and drab hospital environment, he checked out and moved into a hotel room across the street, where he hired nurses to tend to him. He had his doctors visit him there, where he rented all of his favorite funny movies and surrounded himself with beauty and joy and life—and this had amazing impact.

People thought he was a little nuts because although he was very ill, he talked about wanting to feel happy and joyous to help him revive from sickness and stress. Maybe he was a little crazy, but his attitude led to his recovery and the long litany of research that it inspired. I'll share more details about the research for you later, but the point is that when we release our *self* from the junk we think about and say to our *self*, we benefit in tangible ways.

Loma Linda University and Harvard School of Medicine have both conducted decades of research that show clearly that the human body's response to laughter optimizes the functions of various body systems. It affects things like the hormones in the endocrine system, decreasing the levels of cortisol and epinephrine that lead to stress reduction. They've also shown that laughter has a positive effect on modulating components of the immune system, including increased production of antibodies and activation of the body's protective cells, such as T-cells and especially the "natural killer cells" that are activated to kill tumor cells. Laughter causes the body to respond in a way similar to moderate physical exercise and enhances your mood, decreases stress hormones, enhances immune activity, lowers bad cholesterol and systolic blood pressure, and raises good cholesterol (HDL).

The question here is, how do you make it happen? The answer is simple: you direct your mind to engage in the activities of happiness and to just give in to what is funny . . . and enjoy it!

Are you wondering how? I mean, if you're in a horrible mood and your mind has gotten hold of you and you just can't shake that angry feeling from those thoughts of what your boss did to you today, or how your friend acted when you told them something important—whatever it is—what then? This is where your true inner strength comes in and what you say to your *self* matters more than ever. You have absolutely got to grab your *self* and know who is in control. The experience of stress can literally kill us! And the experience of stress is something that is an experience that the mind interprets. Every bit our daily living experience is interpreted by us, every single bit, so why *not* put the best, most favorable spin on things?

When your boss really is a jerk, what do you have to lose by telling your *self* that the person is not nearly as fortunate as you, because at least you know better than to treat someone in that way. Or when that idiot on the road cuts you off, what harm does it do to you to say to your *self* that the poor slob is probably on the way to an emergency appointment to the dentist for an incredibly painful toothache—you have nothing to lose, that's true! BUT on the flip side, if you get mad, allow the frustration to get hold of you, and you explode inside your own thoughts or you scream out loud, you harm your own physiology because you raise your blood pressure, increase your heart rate, constrict your blood vessels, and literally risk having a heart attack as a result.

There's a great book entitled *Is It Worth Dying For?* written by a guy who behaved badly with his own self-talk for decades, and then, in his fifties, had a massive heart attack and wondered what the heck he could have been doing differently. He came to realize in the agony of the attack itself (which can be excruciatingly painful) and during the surgery and the long recovery, that nothing, seriously *nothing*, was worth getting so psychologically bent out of shape about that it was worth dying for.

I have a goal here for you. This is a big, serious goal. I want you to love yourself—for real. I want for you to be able to sit quietly and, at any given moment, talk to yourself in the most genteel manner you can imagine, like you would to someone you really love and care about who is in some form of pain. What are your words to yourself? What would you say to them? How would you comfort them?

Think about it for a minute here.

I'm betting that you thought of someone very dear . . . and you came up with a great script of what to say. I'm also betting that you did a sincerely exquisite job of providing care and of sharing good thoughts and directing them in helpful ways.

Excellent . . . but how about you, now? Can you honestly say that you can, and do, deliver the same quality of messaging and caring to your own self?

Do you have a loving script that you offer to your own mind each day—telling you that you are important and lovely and good, and worthy of every splendid thing you desire in this life?

Your Self Talk Script

Sit very still. Be comfortable, and close your eyes. . . get a clear picture in your mind's eye of your world being peaceful and harmonious . . . you are peaceful and harmonious . . . and here are your words . . . I love who I am . . . I love that I am alive . . . . . . I love my heart . . . I love my mind . . . . .

I am a good, strong, loving human being . . . I am only a human being . . . my faults and my challenges are the beauty of me. I am good in my intentions . . . I am true and gentle . . . . . . I love me . . . I love me to the point of seeing peace all around me and within me and everything that is good is possible. I am capable of happiness . . . happiness that runs deep and is gentle and loving and healthy . . .

Okay, now go to the mirror and we are going to do it again . . . I want you right in front of a mirror that is big enough for you to see your *self* . . . at least your entire head . . . be very still . . . be comfortable . . . . . . keep your eyes open, and actually look right into your own eyes. Look deeply, and see you and your entire world being peaceful and harmonious . . . you are peaceful and harmonious, and here are your words . . . I love who I am . . . I love that I am alive . . . . . . I love my heart, I love my mind . . . I am a good, strong, loving human being . . . I am only a human being . . . my faults and my challenges are the beauty of me, and I am good in my intentions . . . I am true and gentle . . . I love me . . . I love me to the point of seeing peace all around me and within me . . . and everything that is good is possible . . . . I am capable of happiness . . . happiness that runs deep and is gentle and loving and healthy . . .

Keep these words . . . . . . memorize them . . . say them over and over and over . . . and they will become you.

To view the video: www.drdebcarlin.com

THE MAGIC FORMULA OF WHAT TO DO AND HOW TO DO IT

It is my hope that you have been practicing the self talk script I introduced you to and that you are intrigued by the idea of finding yourself more capable of being in control of your thoughts and feeling positive about who you are. When you believe in your own inner goodness and positive qualities, the possibilities for a better life, a life with stress well-managed, becomes yours.

The magic formula of what to do when, and how to do it, is actually very simple. People ask me frequently for the magic formula, the magic pill. Once-upon-a-time-ago, I would tell them that there was no such thing; it was all about the work they needed to do. The problem with that response is that most human beings are not inspired by the idea of having lots of work to do. It makes us feel tired just to even think about it, and that's because the idea of having lots of work to do is overwhelming and there are so many other things we would like to be doing besides working. I had to find my own answers and practical solutions before I could continue to talk about the work.

My desire for the magic formula turned me inward. I began to be very contemplative and thoughtful about the question of magic. What is it anyhow? A true magician will tell you that the hand is faster than the eye, and will also share that everything is an illusion, which means that it is a matter of perception. The funny thing about our perceptions is that we think they are reality—we believe what we experience, what we perceive. We get invested in it and commit to the idea that it is true, whatever *it* is. And we do this all the time, consistently. Sometimes this is helpful and at other times, it is very counter-productive. The problem is that when we have a belief or a perception that is counterproductive, we either don't notice this or we blame the frustration of what it produces on something other than our perception.

To test this, all you have to do is watch people in your own life or on television or in a movie. What you observe, now that you are tuned into this idea, is that people hold tightly to what they see, and most often, we each see the same situation a little differently from one another. We've each had the experience of looking at something, at some situation, and sharing the experience of it with someone, and when talking about it we realize the person had a very different impression of what took place, and even why. What is *that* about?

It's pretty simple, really. From the time we are in the womb, we are exposed to experiences and reactions. Initially, those reactions come from who our mother is. When we are born, we are in the care of people who are adept (in comparison to an infant) at interacting with the world and the many different kinds of people and situations it presents. We are observers. And before we are even verbal, we are watching and creating a network of interpretations about the world: how safe a place it is, how good people are, and how much we can trust.

Psychologists, like the world-famous Jean Piaget, explain that our first stage of development is all about whether or not we can trust the world to be a good and loving place for us to thrive in. The exposure we have to the world and the situations we experience as infants are in terms of emotional reactions—we know how they make us feel. As we develop our mind and our patterns of thinking and also speaking, we come to express what we experience, and we reinforce for ourselves the feelings we have. It's important for a human being to be aligned with our inner thoughts and feelings; otherwise we're very uncomfortable when we're incongruent with the *self*. Things are cock-eyed. We don't tolerate being uncomfortable very well. We crave a match between our thoughts and feelings and that happens when we trust our perceptions.

Some of the work that I do involves responding to requests from insurance companies to handle their tough cases of post-traumatic stress disorder. The insured are individuals who have gone through some sort of incident where something massive happened. They were completely freaked out by it, and they have not been able to re-adjust their think-ing and their feelings from that state of terror. The terror rose up in the moment that they experienced and interpreted something huge.

Every case I have dealt with involves some form of violence and most often violence between people, although there have been cases of natural disasters that also bring on this post-trauma stress. Living through a tornado, a tsunami, or an earthquake is often traumatizing. The experience for the people I work with, however, is about violence caused by people. What's really interesting is that not everyone who was in the violent situation ends up with post-trauma stress. They can have the same situation, same exposure, same threat, same risk, even the same outcome and they survived. What's the difference?

Post-trauma stress is a syndrome, a disorder, where the patient relives the experience both mentally and physically, and it makes them sick and they just cannot shake it—they are captured. It's pretty awful because it is debilitating. The good news, however, is that there is hope.

When people in the same situation are interviewed, and they have had different interpretations about why an event happened, you can hear in the telling of their story the reasons that one person ended up with post-trauma stress and the other did not. The way we describe something tells the listener exactly how we interpreted that something. The people who are suffering from the trauma tell their story with an enormous amount of grief, fear, and anxiety over feelings about not having control—ever—over anything and, most of all, over their own mind. They do not have trust because they didn't expect the situation they were in to erupt, and when it did, the surprise of every element of it became a vivid reality of the unpredictable.

These people often then look for things to be very controllable and somehow predictable. The problem with that is obvious to everyone—the world, and this life experience, is not about predictability, it is about adaptation and flexibility. We have a beautiful, human capability to be flexible and highly adaptive, but our ability is dependent upon our mind to cooperate.

One of the first steps I take when I begin meeting with persons with post-trauma stress is to ask them what they would like for me to know. They universally tell me that they will not talk about the event. I respond by telling them that I am simply available to them to be of assistance, and it is their choice to decide what the conversation is. Usually within the first fifteen minutes, they tell me all about the traumatic incident. I listen with the belief that they are re-telling it in an attempt to understand something new, or to have the listener tell them something new, so that their life can change back to being functional again, and that can only happen if the story can somehow make sense inside their head.

As I listen, I always look for indications of an opportunity to learn about the person and to benefit from this information and embrace it. I always listen until the person has completely finished speaking, and then I ask them why they thought this event happened to them. They always provide several options, and they do this because the person's mind has searched repeatedly for a way to manage the thoughts and the stress they produce, but without a guide out of the deep despair, they get lost and get stuck.

The magic is that the answers are always percolating inside of the person—each and every person—and what is needed is careful listening and a gentle suggestion about the "why" of the circumstance and the potential beauty of the opportunity for them. One hundred percent of the time, this opens up a dialogue about how this dreadful thing happened. The acknowledgment of the degree of how awful it was is enormous and deep, and the offering of the explanation of how the person was chosen for the event because of his or her unique heart and mind and spirit is always a doorway is opened and walked through successfully.

Make no mistake. This is not easy, but it is simple. It then takes time and constant reinforcement to continue to rethink the new inter-pretations of the event in order for a person to be able to move through it and regain confidence. The magic is the inner strength of the human being and the beauty of this life experience to such a passionate degree that there is no way to fail, no way to drop off the positive experience of this life once you experience the control over your own mind, your own thoughts. They are yours—you own them.

This program is about the inner strength that you have and that you need to tap into, and that you need to believe that you can tap into. This is not about anything frivolous or silly; this is about your life and your well-being, and the tapping-in is a fabulous journey for you into the core of your *self.*

BEGINNING THE DANCE
OF BALANCE AT WORK

Whether you are the heir to a fortune or you are a person who needs to find ways to produce income to support your life, we all need to find an equilibrium inside of our head and our heart so that our work life is balanced. When I say "balanced," I mean that whatever is it we do, meets our criteria for being congruent with our being, our entire self. Congruency is an issue for us; it is a part of the human condition, and it is about having consistency within ourselves. When we are out of sync with who we feel we are, with what we see our self as being, and what we expect our self to be doing, we are incongruent. And this means we feel out of alignment and are not having an experience of feeling comfortable and balanced.

Research indicates clearly that for most of us to feel good about what we do, it takes more than the money being paid to us for a job. We actually crave some intrinsic value; we want to feel good about what we accomplish in performing the actual work. For these reasons, it is vital for us to place our mind and our hearts toward the direction of knowing our life purpose and feeling like we understand what we are here to accomplish in this life. At times this can seem impossible and at other times, it will become crystal clear.

So what makes the difference?

The ideas that you've been hearing about and learning in this series have had a lot of core focus on your inner chatter, your *self* talk. Think now about what it is that you say to your *self* about the work that you do, the way in which you spend each work day according to the routine you have established to earn money to have your life afford you the basics and beyond. Are you feeling a sense of genuine pleasure and pride about whatever you do and does your work make you feel good about the person you are at your job? For instance, do you like the title that you have?

When you ask your *self* "What business are you in?" What do you hear your *self* saying in response? Stop here and contemplate for a moment about what you say and the feelings and the thoughts that your words generate. This is really important, even if what you say is: "I just don't know. "

Recall my writings earlier about the investment of time we each make in our work life and the positive correlation that medical data reveals about most heart attacks occurring on Monday mornings. There is another correlation, and it relates to the reality that when we put our self into a position of doing things that are inconsistent with who we are and what we actually want to do, we suffer. We suffer greatly, and we suffer to the point of ill health—even to the point of bringing our life to an early end. No exaggeration here; that's why this topic is so important for us to pay attention to . . . close attention, compassionate attention.

Do you enjoy what you do? Are you utilizing your talents? Are they your favorite talents? If the response is yes, the questions become: Are you where you want to be in using your skill set, and are you reaching your true potential where you are currently? Are people encouraging you? Are you feeling satisfied? And if your answer is no, the question becomes: are you willing to do whatever it takes to step out the misery and save your own life, and do it *now*?

I've worked in hospital settings and in hospice care, and have never heard anyone tell me as they entered the time of having their life close down that they wished they had spent more of their time at their work. I have watched them express regret about the time they wasted doing the wrong work, and that's heartbreaking.

How do you arrive at knowing if your life is on course, if you are living your life purpose and are in balance, and are doing the healthy dance of living your private existence and also thriving in your work life? The answer lies deep within you. And the self talk you've been guided to participate in takes you on the journey to knowing your *self* by tuning in and listening and by really feeling as you hear your thoughts. If you have recoiled from hearing your *self*, the solution is to tune in now—here, today—in this moment, and to pay close attention to what you think.

When I was in my twenties and trying to find my life course, I knew I wanted to be either a physician or a chef or a psychologist. I examined the curriculum for each path of training, I looked at the lifestyle for each, I studied the money you could earn within each, and I looked for role models in each profession. I didn't care for the curriculum and the schedule of becoming a physician, and I felt a desire to do something more intense than being a chef, something that would change people's mind and their hearts. That strong desire made it clear to me that I needed to become a psychologist.

And yet, even in the course of my training and my work, my role has shifted many times with regard to what it is that I do exactly in this line of work. It shifts as I pay close attention to what is happening to me as I do certain aspects of my work and I find there are things I just don't feel satisfied doing. Over the past couple of years, I have felt something inside of me percolating and wanting to bust loose and grow big. It is my desire to reach more people and impact more lives than I have previously. It seems to me that what I do has meaning . . . and I want to help more people receive what I deliver, that is how this book was born.

I have looked around at what happened in my life and at the ways I created a business that allowed me to take time for my personal needs whenever it was truly important to me. That freedom caused me to become more sensitive to what I observe in others and their life choices. So many people feel stuck in their jobs and feel like they have no choices but to stay stuck. I disagree—life is never about keeping you stuck, but is about inviting you to interpret what life presents to you, and being stuck, in my opinion, is an opportunity to twist and shout! Yea, twist in your discomfort and shout out with glee that you're bustin' loose! And don't think you can get away with saying that you are too old to change—never. If you are up and breathing, it is time . . . now.

About a year ago, a woman asked me if I could refer her to someone who could help her son rewrite his resume. I'm very particular who I give referrals to, and I volunteered to take a glance myself and also interview her son so I could determine a best match for him. During the course of the conversation, I was struck with his attitude and his responses because they made it clear to me that it was not his resume that was making it tough for him to get a new job. Instead it was his level of incongruence with what his work experience had been that was in the way.

This was a young man in his late thirties who had been in the retail business for several years, and he hated it. He hated the holiday work time and hated the corporate structure and the hierarchy of bosses and the games played to get profits to increase. It just made him mad. However, he didn't know what else to do, and so he remained there, stuck in a career that caused him a lot of angst. He burrowed in over the years and shut himself off from his inner voices, the ones that told him something was very wrong. And what little volume did get through, he misinterpreted because he was not paying close enough attention, and he came to believe that what was wrong was him, not the job. He felt awful about himself. He spent more than a decade in a depression just sort of floating through the days, which became months and then years. What a waste.

As I recognized what it was that had been taking place, I invited him to consider exploring his talents by thinking about what he really enjoys spending his time doing. This was tough at first. He had turned away from pleasure-seeking because it made him more aware of his discontent, but he allowed me to guide the process. We discovered that what he did find satisfying in retail was the opportunity to help people find the stuff they were looking for. Excellent! I had him take a few online surveys, ones available to anybody on the Internet, to examine his vocational interests—simply Google "vocational interests" and you can do the same. I then engaged him in deep conversations about what he enjoyed and got a sense of how he viewed himself.

I took that information and looked for careers where his personality would be a good fit and where the marketplace appeared secure, so he could enter into something that would produce a respectable income. Within about a month's time, we knew he was a perfect candidate to become an information specialist, a professional librarian. We began exploring the training, had him apply to the academic program he'd need to get through, and he is now happily on his way. Along the path, he was scared and very self-conscious about being close to age forty and feeling like an idiot because he hadn't figured his life out. My response to that is to say that you should ignore your ego in that moment and get going on making things right. He is doing this, and it is amazing and delightful to witness.

There are many more stories to share that are similar, but the point is that it is not ever too late to shift gears with respect to how you earn money and how you spend your time. You just have to envision what you want, how you want to spend your days, what you receive satisfaction from doing, and how you'd like to make it happen. By the way, if you have a life partner, a spouse, kids, or a family to take care of, I understand that this may sound out of reach for you, but out of reach simply means that you need to find the tools to help you make that reach happen. Do it, do whatever it takes to find inner peace and joy. Nothing in this world is worth getting between you and what is good and right for you in order to know your life purpose and do your good life-work as a contribution to the world and to yourself.

Your Self Talk Script

Sit quietly. Breathe . . . be very still. Breathe normally. Steady and easy. Relax. Allow your *self* to envision what it is that you do now for a living, for your work, how it is that produce income.

Stay here with it and attend to what the feelings are inside of you no matter what they are, just hang in here with this and allow it. As you are here, right now, is this what you want? Or do you crave something else? Is there another picture of you coming into view? Can you see your *self* in some glorious light of happiness and fulfillment? Can you feel your *self* in a position where your life makes rich sense and you feel a satisfaction you have been craving?

Pay close attention to this and extend compassion and patience to your *self*. You can make anything happen . . . . . . reach down into your core and feel the strength within you . . . it is there. It is your self love, it is your dedication to who it is that you want to be . . . allow it. You can find it and obtain it, just keep what it is in your mind's eye and know that where your thoughts go, your energy flows.

Breathe, relax, envision, commit. It'll unfold, if you allow it.

To view the video: www.drdebcarlin.com

"We've got to remember,
Our work is serious...we aren't."

—CLINT EASTWOOD

SELF-ASSESSMENT
Self-Determination & Resolution

It is important to your *self* to be really tuned into the level of your ability to commit to being resolved to make decisions and to follow through on them.

This is your life; this is all about you . . . what do you know about your *self*?

Answer honestly. If you don't, then this is just a silly game that is a waste of time, especially yours.

1 = not at all   9 = all the way

1. I am determined to accomplish what I identify as important to me.

1   2   3   4   5   6   7   8   9

2. I am clear about what it is that is important to me.

1   2   3   4   5   6   7   8   9

3. I routinely set goals.

1   2   3   4   5   6   7   8   9

4. I accomplish the goals I set before I make new ones.

1   2   3   4   5   6   7   8   9

5. I am very good at establishing goals, setting them, accomplishing them, and then moving on.

1   2   3   4   5   6   7   8   9

When thinking of goals, do you include resolutions you make at the beginning of each new year?   Yes   No

Have you made resolutions for the current year?   Yes   No

Are you sticking to them?   Yes   No

PLAN OF ACTION TOOL
Self-Determination & Resolution

What are the goals you set for yourself last year?

Did you accomplish them?   Yes   No

Why and how . . . OR . . . why not?

What are the goals you set for yourself this year?

Are you on the path towards accomplishing them?   Yes   No

What is the path?

What are you willing to do to make it happen?

SELF-ASSESSMENT
Freedom of Movement

When you focus your attention on an infant, you see the movements they make as unrestricted. The foot goes easily up to the mouth; the hands and arms move about the body in wide-ranging circles. From the time we're born, we are flexible, bendable, and able to move in lots of directions—much like the yogis do as they fascinate us with their flexibility.

Why is it that we transition from being so flexible into becoming rigid?

Why do we become restricted?

Maybe you are not . . . let's see.

The opening question for you here is: how well do you move? Think carefully and reply to the questions.

Answer honestly . . . if you don't, then this is just a silly game that is a waste of time—especially yours.

1 = not at all   9 = all the way

1. I have an extremely flexible body.

    1   2   3   4   5   6   7   8   9

2. I am able to move my body without restriction or pain anywhere.

    1   2   3   4   5   6   7   8   9

3. I am completely functional with no awkwardness or stiffness in any part of my body.

    1   2   3   4   5   6   7   8   9

4. I can move my arms with full range of movement.

    1   2   3   4   5   6   7   8   9

5. I can move my hips with full range of movement.

    1   2   3   4   5   6   7   8   9

6. I can move my legs with full range of movement and zero pain in my knees.

    1   2   3   4   5   6   7   8   9

7. I can move and walk, and my feet are comfortable with no pain, no aches, no problems.

    1   2   3   4   5   6   7   8   9

8. I am confident the people in my work life would agree with my assessment.

    1   2   3   4   5   6   7   8   9

9. I am confident that the people in my personal life would agree with my assessment.

    1   2   3   4   5   6   7   8   9

PLAN OF ACTION TOOL
Movement Reflection

As we age, we accumulate experiences, feeling, and memories. They develop into perceptions. Combined, they work their way around in our mind, into our heart, and throughout our body. They cause us to be comfortable, and they cause us to feel uncomfortable. We grow to be uptight. We become tight, tense, rigid—holding on to whatever it is that is roaming around inside that we're not tapped into.

Look around the room at the way people walk. The majority of adults have some sort of gait disorder. Why? A portion of the answer is weight, some of it is lack of exercise, and some of it is emotional baggage.

It almost doesn't matter what it is; the point is to do something to regain your freedom—your freedom of movement. Or was your score perfect exactly where it is?

To begin, we need to work with an expert who can guide us through routines and exercises that will be of specific help to our body issues. Pilates and yoga are both perfect routines. We begin here with the story of Pilates. I insert the story to clear misperceptions and to entice your motivation.

About Yoga *(Straight from Wikipedia)*

HISTORY

Pilates was designed by Joseph Pilates, a physical-culturist born in Mönchengladbach, Germany in 1883. He developed a system of exercises during the first half of the 20th century which were intended to strengthen the human mind and body. Joseph Pilates believed that mental and physical health are interrelated.

He had practiced many of the physical training regimes which were available in Germany in his youth, and it was out of this context that he developed his own work, which has clear connections with the physical culture of the late nineteenth century such as the use of specially invented apparatuses and the claim that the exercises could cure illness.

It is also related to the tradition of "corrective exercise" or "medical gymnastics" which is typified by Pehr Henrik Ling.

Joseph Pilates published two books in his lifetime which related to his training method: *Your Health: A Corrective System of Exercising That Revolutionizes the Entire Field of Physical Education* (1934) and *Return to Life through Contrology* (1945). In common with early C20 physical culture, Pilates had an extremely high regard for the Greeks and the physical prowess demonstrated in their Gymnasium.

The first generation of students, many of them dancers, studied with Joseph Pilates and went on to open studios and teach the method are collectively known as The Elders and the most prominent include: Romana Kryzanowska, Kathy Grant, Jay Grimes, Ron Fletcher, Maja Wollman, Mary Bowen, Carola Treir, Bob Seed, Eve Gentry, Bruce King, Lolita San Miguel and Mary Pilates (the niece of Joseph and Clara). Modern day Pilates styles, both "traditional" and "contemporary", are derived from the teaching of these first generation students. The method was originally confined to the few and normally practiced in a specialized studio, but with time this has changed and Pilates can now be found in community centers, gyms and physiotherapy rooms as well as in hybrid practice such as yogilates and in newly developed forms such as the Menezes Method. The "traditional" form still survives and there are also a variety of "contemporary" schools, such as Stott Pilates, which have adapted the system in different ways.

THE PILATES METHOD

The Pilates method seeks to develop controlled movement from a strong core and it does this using a range of apparatuses to guide and train the body. Joe Pilates originally developed his method as mat exercises (his 1945 *Return to Life* teaches 34 of these), but, in common with many other physical culture systems from the first part of the twentieth century, he used several pieces of apparatus to help people "get the method in their bodies." Each piece of apparatus has its own repertoire of exercises and most of the exercises done on the various pieces of Pilates apparatus are resistance training since they make use of springs to provide additional resistance. Using springs results in "progressive resistance," meaning the resistance increases as the spring is stretched.

The most widely used piece of apparatus, and probably the most important, is the Reformer, but other apparatus used in a traditional Pilates studio include the Cadillac (also called the Trapeze Table), the

High (or electric) Chair, the Wunda Chair, the Baby Chair, and the Ladder Barrel, the Spine Corrector (Step Barrel) and Small Barrel. Lesser used apparati include the Magic Circle, Guillotine Tower, the Pedi-Pole, and the Foot Corrector.

In contemporary Pilates other props are used, including small weighted balls, foam rollers, large exercise balls, rotating disks, and resistance bands. Some of the traditional apparati have been adapted for use in contemporary Pilates (e.g., splitting the pedal on the wunda chair). Some contemporary schools, such as the British Body Control Pilates, work primarily on the mat with these smaller props, enabling people to study the method without a full studio.

Currently the Pilates Method is divided into two camps, Classical/Authentic Pilates or Contemporary/Modern Pilates. Classical/Authentic Pilates teach the exercises in an order that does not vary from lesson to lesson. Teachers of this style of Pilates seek to stay close to Joseph Pilates's original work and generally use equipment that is built to his specifications. Most classically trained teachers will have studied the complete system of exercises and can generally trace their training back to Joseph Pilates through one of his proteges. Contemporary/Modern Pilates breaks the method down into various parts and the order of the exercises varies from lesson to lesson with many changes made to the original exercises.

Principles

Philip Friedman and Gail Eisen, two students of Romana Kryzanowska, published the first modern book on Pilates, *The Pilates Method of Physical and Mental Conditioning*, in 1980 and in it they outlined six "principles of Pilates." These have been widely adopted—and adapted—by the wider community. The original six principles were: concentration, control, center, flow, precision and breathing.

Concentration

Pilates demands intense focus: "You have to concentrate on what you're doing. All the time. And you must concentrate on your entire body." This is not easy, but in Pilates the way that exercises are done is more important than the exercises themselves. In 2006, at the Parkinson Center of the Oregon Health and Science University in Portland, Oregon, the concentration factor of the Pilates method was being studied in providing relief from the degenerative symptoms of Parkinson's disease.

Control

"Contrology" was Joseph Pilates' preferred name for his method and it is based on the idea of muscle control. "Nothing about the Pilates Method is haphazard. The reason you need to concentrate so thoroughly is so you can be in control of every aspect of every moment." All exercises are done with control with the muscles working to lift against gravity and the resistance of the springs and thereby control the movement of the body and the apparatus. "The Pilates Method teaches you to be in control of your body and not at its mercy."

Centering

In order to attain control of your body you must have a starting place: the center. The center is the focal point of the Pilates Method. Many Pilates teachers refer to the group of muscles in the center of the body—encompassing the abdomen, lower and upper back, hips, buttocks and inner thighs—the "powerhouse." All movement in Pilates should begin from the powerhouse and flow outward to the limbs.

Flow or Efficiency of Movement

Pilates aims for elegant sufficiency of movement, creating flow through the use of appropriate transitions. Once precision has been achieved, the exercises are intended to flow within and into each other in order to build strength and stamina. In other words, the Pilates technique asserts that physical energy exerted from the center should coordinate movements of the extremities: Pilates is flowing movement outward from a strong core.

Precision

Precision is essential to correct Pilates: "concentrate on the correct movements each time you exercise, lest you do them improperly and thus lose all the vital benefits of their value." The focus is on doing one precise and perfect movement, rather than many halfhearted ones. Pilates is here reflecting common physical culture wisdom: "You will gain more strength from a few energetic, concentrated efforts than from a thousand listless, sluggish movements." The goal is for this precision to eventually become second nature, and carry over into everyday life as grace and economy of movement.

Breathing

Breathing is important in the Pilates method. In *Return to Life*, Pilates devotes a section of his introduction specifically to breathing. "Bodily house-cleaning with blood circulation" He saw considerable value in increasing the intake of oxygen and the circulation of this oxygenated blood to every part of the body. This he saw as cleansing and invigorating. Proper full inhalation and complete exhalation were key to this. "Pilates saw forced exhalation as the key to full inhalation." He advised people to squeeze out the lungs as you would wring a wet towel dry.

In Pilates exercises, you breathe out with the effort and in on the return. In order to keep the lower abdominals close to the spine; the breathing needs to be directed laterally, into the lower ribcage. Pilates breathing is described as a posterior lateral breathing, meaning that the practitioner is instructed to breathe deep into the back and sides of his or her rib cage. When practitioners exhale, they are instructed to note the engagement of their deep abdominal and pelvic floor muscles and maintain this engagement as they inhale. Pilates attempts to properly coordinate this breathing practice with movement, including breathing instructions with every exercise. "Above all, learn to breathe correctly."

We breathe on average around 18,000 breaths per day. Posterior lateral breathing is a way of breathing that facilitates bibasal expansion of the ribcage, this encourages the breath to travel down into the lower lungs and cleanse the blood by the exchange of oxygen with carbon dioxide. To understand this concept properly you have to first learn to expand and release the ribcage without deliberately breathing in or out. The in-breath (inhalation) and out-breath (exhalation) should occur instinctively as a result of the conscious expansion and release of the ribcage.

This is how you would do this: You place your hands on your lower ribs with you thumbs facing the back of your ribcage, try not to think of breathing, relax your upper abdominals and expand your ribcage to the side against the soft resistance of your hands. Release the expansion of the ribcage by first melting away the area of the clavicles. You can also try this with a scarf around the lower ribcage. You will not be able to expand and release the ribcage effectively if you try to contract your abdominal muscles to expand the ribcage and if you try to contract the ribcage instead of first release it.

Now you should try to duplicate this action with conscious breathing in and breathing out. The in-breath (let it come) widens the ribcage laterally, posteriorly, and superiorly in the ratio of 60:30:10. That is 60% laterally, 30% posteriorly and 10% superiorly. The effect of this ratio of distribution is felt mainly as a back activity. The out-breath (gradually let it out) exits the body first through the gradual and gentle release of tension (intention) in the upper chest and breastbone area, without collapsing the front of the ribcage, and terminates through the activation of the power engine.

Power Engine or Powerhouse

Pilates emphasizes the concepts of core strength and stabilization. Students are taught the concepts of core strength and stabilization, as well as to use your "powerhouse" throughout life's daily activities. As Joseph Pilates called it, your "powerhouse" is the center of your body or your core and if strengthened, it offers a solid foundation for any movement. This power engine is a muscular network which provides the basic control and stability in the lumbopelvic region, which furthermore consists of the Pelvic floor muscles, the Transversus, the Multifidus, the diaphragm, the muscles of the inner thigh, and the muscles encircling the sitting bone area.

You activate the power engine effectively by hollowing of the deep abdominals and pelvic floor muscles ("Deep muscle corset"), by drawing the navel back into the spine in a zipping-up motion, from the pubic bone to the breast bone thereby engaging the heels, the back of the inner thighs, the deep lower back muscles, and the muscles surrounding the sitting bones and tailbone area without inhibiting the natural function of the diaphragm–that is without holding your breath either from lifting the chest upwards or contracting the chest.

Apart from providing core control and stability to the lumbopelvic region, in the sitting position the power engine elevates the torso and places the center of gravity at its highest and most efficient position; in prone position it elongates the body bi-directionally to reduce weight in the upper body; in supine position it elongates the body bi-directionally and places the center of gravity again at its highest and most efficient position.

The Power Engine opens up the vertical dimension of the body by grounding the pelvis to the earth and by elevating the spine towards the sky, much like a tree; the pelvis being the root and the branches being the spine.

Neutral Spine

The human spine is made up of a complex chain of ligaments, fascia, bone, muscles and inter-vertebral discs which is required to be both stable and flexible. The natural curves of the spine (cervical and lumbar) are interdependent and whilst each curve supports the other, any deviation can also affect the other. In Pilates the aim throughout most stabilizing exercises is to maintain these natural curves and create a neutral position for each joint that is close to its optimal alignment. In this neutral position the deep postural muscles of the spine (Multifidus and Transversus Abdominus) can be recruited effectively, thus strengthening each vertebrae in alignment to reduce stress on the spinal tissues and inter-vertebral discs. A neutral spine in the semi-supine position involves the alignment of the head, shoulders, thorax, spine and pelvis to ensure that all sections of the body are in their ideal place. The head should be centered, with a small head cushion under the head to prevent the chin from lifting and the neck extending. The head and neck should be gently lengthening away from the shoulders. The shoulders are relaxed with a sense of a gently drawing down action of the shoulder blades to stabilize the scapular and release neck tension.

Precautions

Pilates during pregnancy has been claimed to be a highly valuable and beneficial form of exercise, but the use of Pilates in pregnancy should only be undertaken under guidance of a fully trained expert.

The origins of yoga are every bit as helpful to understand as those of Pilates. Before we engage in a program, we ought to educate ourselves about what we're getting into and then find the best instruction available. What follows is what Wikipedia has to share with us that I have found to be applicable. The practice is centuries old and has many divisions—what you'll find here is the more Americanized version.

RECEPTION IN THE WEST

Yoga came to the attention of an educated western public in the mid-19th century along with other topics of Hindu philosophy. The first Hindu teacher to actively advocate and disseminate aspects of Yoga to a Western audience was Swami Vivekananda, who toured Europe and the United States in the 1890s.

In the West, the term "yoga" is today typically associated with Hatha Yoga and its asanas (postures) or as a form of exercise. In the 1960s, western interest in Hindu spirituality reached its peak, giving rise to a great number of Neo-Hindu schools specifically advocated to a western public. Among the teachers of Hatha yoga who were active in the west in this period were B.K.S. Iyengar, K. Pattabhi Jois, and Swami Vishnu-devananda, and Swami Satchidananda. A second "yoga boom" followed in the 1980s, as Dean Ornish, a follower of Swami Satchidananda, connected yoga to heart health, legitimizing yoga as a purely physical system of health exercises outside of counter culture or esotericism circles, and unconnected to a religious denomination.

Kundalini Yoga, considered an advanced form of yoga and meditation, was on the whole a secretive and misunderstood technology—it was not widely taught by any master teachers outside of India until Yogi Bhajan (Siri Singh Sahib) brought his understanding of the teachings to the United States in 1969.

There has been an emergence of studies investigating yoga as a complementary intervention for cancer patients. Yoga is used for treatment of cancer patients to decrease depression, insomnia, pain, and fatigue and increase anxiety control. Mindfulness Based Stress Reduction (MBSR) programs include yoga as a mind-body technique to reduce stress. A study found that after seven weeks the group treated with yoga reported significantly less mood disturbance and reduced stress compared to the control group. Another study found that MBSR had showed positive effects on sleep anxiety, quality of life, and spiritual growth.

Yoga has also been studied as a treatment for schizophrenia. Yoga is found to improve cognitive functions and reduce stress in schizophrenia, a condition associated with cognitive deficits and stress-related relapse. In one study, at the end of four months those patients treated with yoga were better in their social and occupational functions and quality of life.

The three main focuses of Hatha yoga (exercise, breathing, and meditation) make it beneficial to those suffering from heart disease. Overall, studies of the effects of yoga on heart disease suggest that yoga may reduce high blood pressure, improve symptoms of heart failure, enhance cardiac rehabilitation, and lower cardiovascular risk factors.

Long-term yoga practitioners in the United States have reported musculoskeletal and mental health improvements, as well reduced symptoms of asthma in asthmatics. Regular yoga practice increases brain GABA levels and is shown to improve mood and anxiety more than other metabolically matched exercises, such as jogging or walking. Implementation of the Kundalini Yoga Lifestyle has shown to help substance abuse addicts increase their quality of life according to psychological questionnaires like the Behavior and Symptom Identification Scale and the Quality of Recovery Index.

http://en.wikipedia.org/wiki/Pilates, accessed May, 2012

Use this space here to write the exercises specific to your body issues as you tuned in to what they are.

Include the recommended schedule for doing them.

Envision that the goal is to be upright, strong, and centered.

SELF-ASSESSMENT
Beginning Work–Life Integration

If you find yourself thinking that you can easily separate your personal life from your work life, I invite you to think again about whether your life is out of balance a little differently than you have before. It is important to be contemplative about the wholeness of who we are as humans and understand whether we have a successful integration of each aspect of our personality. It is important to realize how we interpret the experiences we have and how we behave as a result of this. When we divide our *self* by segmenting our *self* into pieces and believe that we should compartmentalize what we do into pockets, we fracture our core and enter a pathway towards disintegration at many levels.

The partner who steps outside of her or his monogamous relationship, the worker who engages in espionage, and the friend who talks badly and reveals secrets shared in confidence, all engage in actions that lead to inner conflict and prompt weird behavior as the persons tries to internally justify what they are doing.

The same is true in the way we try to resist blending our personal and work life. I first became aware of this when I was working on a business deal that I thought was moving along quite well, but at the closing of it I was told by one of the associates not to take personally what was going to happen because it was just business, nothing personal. The commentary stuck in my mind and I came to recognize it as code for "you're about to get nailed, to get cheated, and someone is trying to take himself off the hook of guilt by proclaiming it is merely business."

Business is very personal. We take it to heart when we get hired, fired, or evaluated, and also when we get included or excluded from a meeting, a team, an event, or a decision. There is nothing about business that is not personal. Period. This works both ways—we are each a whole person. We take our head and our heart along with us wherever it is that we travel to. If there is trouble at home, it spills over into the workplace and everybody knows it. Try to cover it up and people talk about our weird behavior. If you become ill, you are sick both at home and at work. Where we go, our stuff follows.

The opening question for you here is: how well-integrated are you between your personal and work life? Think about your answer as you reply to the questions that follow.

Answer honestly . . . if you don't, this is just a silly game that is a waste of time.

1 = not at all   9 = all the way

1. I am an integrationist between my work and personal life.

    1   2   3   4   5   6   7   8   9

2. I am a separatist between my work and personal life.

    1   2   3   4   5   6   7   8   9

3. I am completely functional, no awkwardness at all in the way I deal with personal and work life.

    1   2   3   4   5   6   7   8   9

4. I am confident the people in my work life would agree with my assessment.

    1   2   3   4   5   6   7   8   9

5. I am confident that the people in my personal life would agree with my assessment.

    1   2   3   4   5   6   7   8   9

PLAN OF ACTION TOOL
Which Parts of You Are Where?

Look at the pictures below. Pretend the picture symbolizes you.

    Visualize what parts of you are where, that is,

        which parts of you are at your work life,

        and what parts of you are at your personal life,

        and what parts of you are integrated into both?

Use color to help you see this clearly. Use the colored pencils and just point to or circle the various parts. One color is for your work life and one color is your personal life. If colors overlap, it's ok . . . this is simply your own representation of your inner perceptions.

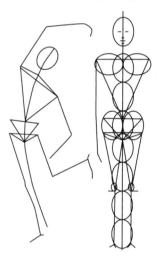

    Take a moment and think about what you just created in the way of a visual for yourself.

    Is it the best you?   Yes   No

    In order to really know what the best you is and can be, you need to be overtly aware of your values and your rules. List here what your values and rules are.

PLAN OF ACTION TOOL
Your Passions

Your values and rules are closely tied to your passions. Getting a clear and tangible picture of your passions is essential because our passions drive us. Fill the categories below.

What I love
(What I must absolutely have in my life)

What I hate
(What I won't stand for in my life)

What excites and drives me
(What I am most passionate about)

What I am committed to
(The results I must achieve)

As you look at what you have listed and also looked at how you colored the picture of yourself and the ways you have identified the parts of you that are invested in your personal life and your life, think of how you need improvement in both your personal and work life and list them. Just start with 5 in each.

PERSONAL AREAS OF IMPROVEMENT

1.

2.

3.

4.

5.

PROFESSIONAL AREAS OF IMPROVEMENT

1.

2.

3.

4.

5.

Now look at which one you have more to write about, your personal or your work life—

Or are they 50–50?

PLAN OF ACTION TOOL
Examine Your Passions & Values

Success without fulfillment is failure.—TONY ROBBINS

When you examine your values and your passions, what you love and cannot live without, you must see that you are willing to commit time and energy there. *You want an extraordinary life!* The quality of your life is equal to the power of your focus.

Whether you love him or you don't know him, Tony Robbins is the world's authority on success and life mastery. He's been reaching for it for more than forty years and has been teaching it and talking about it for more than thirty of them. His core pitch is about our focus. I've heard him say: "Focus is the ultimate power that can change the way we think, the way we feel, and what we do in any moment. When we change our focus, we change our lives. What we focus on determines the direction in which we move." This is true and is basic social psychology.

You must learn to control your focus. You cannot do this unless you know your *self* well enough to identify what is important and how it all works together to make your life experience whole. You need to take the time for your *self* in order to make this happen.

You can argue that our perception of time is many things, and you can go on a scientific or philosophical bender. What it boils down to is that time involves emotion. The meaning of time to us is completely influenced by our feelings . . . time is a way of looking at life that involves our emotional state.

Think about it. The clock will tell you actual time, but how you feel will give you completely different experiences of that same frame of time. A minute can feel like an eternity when you're stressed or you are not fulfilled, but when you love what you are doing, and you're thoroughly engaged into it, time flies by . . . and seems not even to be a factor, as if it doesn't exist.

An Extraordinary Life Is One That Keeps You Consistently Fulfilled

This is important. A life worth living is a life that has engaged and occupied the mind and the heart. It is a life that captures your attention and your focus, so that no matter what the stress is, you find your *self* and you command the time for you to grab hold . . . of you, your mind, and your physiological state. You never lose sight of the fact that your values are intact and you have rules, passions, and motivations that cannot be compromised.

You need a plan for your life that provides balance so all the areas of your life will work together in harmony. We begin with awareness and follow with focus, as demonstrated in the previous pages.

Without a plan, we increase the experience of:

> fear and anxiety, because we know something is out of sync and we've not grabbed hold of it;

> and having only momentary pleasure, because we're looking to relieve the fear and anxiety.

Both are equally harmful because both can be seductive enough to distract us and cause us to lose focus on our values and commitments. Think about the ways in which you've experienced both—to your detriment.

Awareness, focus, and a plan guide us to fulfillment, an extraordinary life experience.

"Live as if you were to die tomorrow.
Learn as if you were to live forever."

—MAHATMA GANDHI

Blueprint for a Successfully Intentional & Integrated Life

In the last section, which is all about "The Basics," the foundation was laid for the Blueprint work to begin. The idea is to let yourself envision your life as the biggest and best project you'll ever take on. You want to build it right which means to build it strong, durable, smart, beautiful, and intentional. With help from Erikson, you have the advantage of gaining another perspective on what your life experience has been thus far and where it is that you now find yourself. You will also want clarity about how best to propel yourself forward.

You don't need to be a stage theorist to understand that life has a series of events that we all share and that can be viewed as stages. These are simply time frames and developmental phases that we move through, and depending upon what happens to us in each phase, we end up being either stuck or propelled forward. Either way, we can benefit from pausing long enough to get a few thoughts and feelings sorted through to provide the perspective we need to move ahead in our life and feeling empowered and confident about who we are and where we have come from.

Regardless of your life circumstances, you have reason to be determined and feel confident about being able to have the life you are eager to have. We all come from essentially nothing, and it is up to each one of us to make sense out of what takes place each day and to put a powerful, positive spin on it with a smart strategy so we can continue to survive and desire to thrive.

Using the Blueprint as a tool, keep Erikson in your thoughts, and allow yourself the time to let loose and do your self-portrait, a few times—with the idea in mind that it is not an exercise of artistry, but is one of self expression, a private self expression that can be powerful for you. You simply need to allow it.

Additionally, gaining some new insights about how your mind prefers to work is very powerful. Appreciating the style of your brain facilitates your learning, your communications, and all of your relationships and productive actions. Knowing your brain style is analogous to knowing the English language. The more ability you have and the more articulate you are, the more opportunity you have to gain satisfaction.

The brain work also helps us develop further a genuine appreciation for just how powerful the mind really is. It is beyond any universe or a galaxy that we've yet seen; it is simply massive. With this massiveness that is *us*, we have incredible capacity for whatever, and I sincerely mean—whatever!

The Series 16 videos are designed to provide additional information to lead you into understanding who you are and what you want, alongside developing an appreciation for how to make it happen. As we begin this section, become reflective about how you envision what you're building here in the way of your best life yet, with a new appreciation for who you are and what your life experience has been thus far.

Reexamining the Assessments

The best use of a test is the re-test. Now is the time to retake the assessments you did earlier. Retake them on the same page where you initially did, but this time using a different color pencil so you can track any shifts and then use this open space to write your thoughts with respect to any shifts in ideas, frustrations, motivations, and inspirations.

You will find a color code key on the Blueprint to help you track changes.

Assessments to review and retake:

    Brain Power

    Self-Determination

    Freedom of Movement

    Work-Life Integration

Understanding Maslow
1908–1970

Abraham Maslow, like Erikson, was a world-renowned psychologist. He is best known for the creation of a theory that emphasizes focusing on the positive components of the life experience of each person instead of the negatives. He was influenced by an era when psychology and psychiatry placed the primary emphasis on the symptoms of illness a person had rather than an individual's potential.

As is true for all theorists, whose own life experience shapes their perspective on human character and how the mind works, Maslow developed his theory, in part, as a reaction to the frustration he felt in trying to understand how humans behave when using the models of symptoms of illness to examine disorders of the mind and of the personality. His thinking took shape into what has become known as Humanistic Psychology. It is a theory that is thought to be kinder and gentler than other perspectives about how human beings behave. Humanistic psychologists believe that every person has a strong desire to realize his or her full potential in order to reach a level of what they call self-actualization.

To demonstrate that humans are not simply blindly reacting to situations, but are indeed trying to accomplish something greater, Maslow studied mentally healthy individuals instead of people with serious psychological issues. His theory is that people have peak experiences, i.e., high points in life when they are in harmony with their *self* and surroundings.

Maslow describes the self-actualized individual as being very clear and conscious about reality and about ideas of right vs. wrong and truth vs. falsehood. They are comfortable spending time alone and in balance with being with others. They can be described as interdependent as opposed to being dependent in their relationships. They are viewed as being centered, grounded, and having a strong, reliable, and accurate sense of self. Most typically, they have a circle of deep, genuine relationships, as opposed to a large, superficial network.

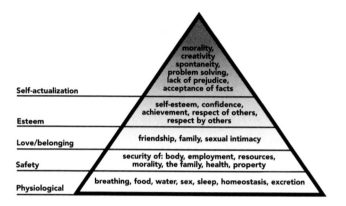

Similar to the manner in which Erikson described the human experience in a series of stages, Maslow established a model of humans' hierarchy of needs that teaches us that each stage of psychological growth is based upon fulfilling five levels of basic needs. Our interactions with the world affect our motivation and personality in very tangible ways as we interpret the events of our daily living according to our perception of the fulfillment of physiological and psychological needs.

If we are hungry, the experience will absorb us until we have that need met. Hunger is foremost and distracts us from being able to focus on anything else until we're satiated. Even our educational system in the United States understands that there is not much benefit extending academic material to students if they are hungry; we need nourishment if we are going to be asked to concentrate. The same is true for the issue of safety. For instance, to make this point with a clear and extreme example, we cannot possibly be asked to read the *Wall Street Journal* if we are in the middle of a home invasion or a bank robbery.

Life is an enormous experience; it is complex to the degree that we have many components to attend to. Life is busy and there are a multitude of distractions for us. It is important for us to keep in the forefront of our mind that unless we manage these components as natural parts of the life experience and focus on what we are eager to attain, we will never get to the point of ultimate attainment, what Maslow calls self-actualization and what I refer to as excellence. Both are a reach, a striving for, something that works in the direction of keeping all things balanced and attended to healthfully.

The Big Question for You Is:

The question for you to contemplate, for each of us to consider is: what sort of life do you want to have?

What do you really desire?

What stage of Maslow's model do you see yourself in? When we write our life experience, our life story . . . where do you want to land?

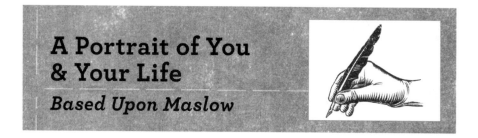

A Portrait of You & Your Life
Based Upon Maslow

Each stage of our development is based upon our interactions with the world, with how we interpret the events of our daily living, with what we do in our mind with our perceptions, and with how we write our life experience—that is our life story.

With the idea of self-actualization in mind, create where you are and where your life is, in relationship to self-actualization.

WHY I TOOK THIS JOURNEY AND HOW IT SAVED MY LIFE

It is impossible to be genuine about something unless you are passionate about it, and passion comes from a place of feeling. And the passion about our life is precious. I never feel hesitant about sharing the reality that I experience regarding how precious life is, how brief it is, and how the most essential portion of it is the love we know while we are here.

When I mention love, I am not just waxing philosophical or being romantic. I am also thinking of the hard evidence we have in medicine and psychology about the power of love—love being that bond, that connection, that emotion that we feel for one another. It begins before we can even speak.

Back during a time in our history when unwed mothers were often placed into institutional settings to spare their families the social strife of an unplanned pregnancy, babies were born into those places with an environment that was not what we'd describe as warm and nurturing. In fact, they were often cold and lifeless. There was a different theme in our society about how to manage these young mothers and their babies, and it often entailed treating these moms as though they were mentally ill.

The babies were often taken away from the mothers after birth and cared for by a staff. The story is that some babies, who were placed into bland, stark cribs, were not held and cuddled, but were bottle fed with a hand that reached into the crib to pass the liquid into the mouth almost mechanically. Deprived of maternal or any other individual attention, the infants didn't develop the sucking response, and as a result, failed to survive. Notably, at a much later time, theorists examined this pattern and concluded that without human touch, the experience of eye contact, the warmth of another human body, and the beating of another heart, these infants were not motivated to suck and take nourishment. The world to them was not anything to engage with—it was stark and the babies died. This is a phenomenon known as the "failure to thrive."

We see a similar situation with the elderly when they come to feel useless and unwelcome by the world and by their loved ones. When they come to believe they have no value, they often stop eating, and they also fail to thrive. These stories are important because they speak to the life and death consequences of love and attachment as a part of The Human Condition.

You've heard the expression that someone *died of a broken heart*. It is a truth, and it happens more often than we can ever feel comfortable about. Love runs deep; it causes us to do all sorts of things that surprise us—we've all experienced that reality, each one of us, in some way, at some level.

My mother and father were truly exceptional people. They were amazing—very loving, very smart, highly intuitive, and massively kind. They were also very much in love with one another. When my father died about fifteen years ago, I was terrified that my mother would die as a result. I was determined to do whatever I could to refresh her sense of life and being needed by deepening my need for her and expanding my attachment to her. We spent increasingly more time with one another, and we even worked together in new and creative ways that I came up with routinely. I had her re-teaching me a lot of what she had taught me in previous years, but now with a new surge of energy and interest between us. It was very difficult for her to survive the passing of my dad, but she did it and she did it knowing how much I needed her in this world. We spent more than a decade enjoying life on this new pathway.

And then, as she turned 80 and began to get into her mid-80s, there were health issues and it was tough, but we knew our routines and managed most of it. But then there were a series of incidents, and she ended up with a horrible infection and an autoimmune disease that initiated a rare kind of anemia. For the last couple years of her life, we spent a lot of time in physician offices and hospitals. It became our routine and the people there became close to us. It was our reality. I slowly shut off my business and we spent 100 percent of our time together, pretty much side by side—literally.

I loved the time with her and knew it was precious even though I didn't know what sort of time frame we had for all that was happening. She was such a beautiful lady, both physically and with respect to her sparkling personality, it was often hard to realize how ill she really was. Even staff commented consistently about her vibrance and beauty. It was lovely and also remarkable. I managed the stress that I was feeling by holding close in my mind the opportunity of getting to spend such valuable time with my remaining parent.

The time was unusual in many ways, but also typical, because as a mother and daughter there were the commonplace struggles and power issues, including themes of my reactions to bossiness and all that childhood stuff that never really fades. And at a time when I had hoped that perhaps we would have more time, which is what we always want with someone that we love, she died.

When we were at home the few days before this happened, it was tough because she just didn't feel well, and there was a lot of contact with our doctors. We had nurses and therapists who made house calls. We were trying some new medications and we thought that we had more time, but I ended up calling 911 and returning us to the hospital, and had to manage once again the medical terrain and the trauma that this presents for every one of us. I managed my stress at that time by staying proactive about getting what I believed she needed medically and emotionally and spiritually.

It was particularly odd, though, because as the hours passed and I sat in her room next to her bed, holding her hands, I had the feeling of wanting to hold her close like she had held me when I was a child. I just wanted to love her as much as any human can love another human—this lovely woman who had given me my life and now was slipping out of mine. I recall sitting there and knowing that if I would allow it, I would take my last breath when she took hers, and knowing this frightened me, because I knew somewhere inside of me about the connection between people and the connection of the mind and the body. And I knew that my thoughts were causing my body to feel things I had never experienced before. It was really strange and really powerful and it felt like I could just disintegrate. It was pretty awful. My mind was not my own in those hours, and I knew that somehow I needed to recapture myself. I needed to remember what I guide others to know and do. I needed to tap into my inner strength, the strength my parents had cultivated in me.

In the last seven or eight hours of my mother's life, I had to steel myself from my own grief and tend only to what was happening to her. And so I was at her bedside, to talk and watch and listen and to pray. My mom and I shared our faith and we prayed with one another for years. It was a wonderful experience and it added a quality to our knowing of one another that was rich. And when this lovely woman took her last breaths, I sat and felt stunned, completely stunned. I remained there for some long period of time. It was daybreak when I walked outside. I felt like I needed to check into the hospital, because the feeling of being completely stressed, overwhelmed, depleted, scared, and immediately lonesome was enormous.

I walked around and just drifted. I went to the beach and stared into space. I went to our home and sat in a state of shock for a day, just sitting and feeling everything and then also nothing. And then, I began to relive every moment as though I had some form of post-trauma stress. And then I began crying and it felt like that would never end. In my tears, I could not envision ever *not* crying because with the loss of my mother, so much of my life was now done. I had lost my family and so many others. What was left for me?

My mother died on April 4th. My birthday falls on April 6th. Every year of my life, my family celebrated my birthday with great enthusiasm. It was the tradition in my family that we value life and make a big deal out of the date of our birth and give thanks for our many blessings. And so, as the hours passed over those short couple of days, I arrived at a place of awareness that I needed to remember the value my family had placed on life—and that my mother wanted, more than anything, for me to outlive her and to be happy and healthy. I had to find a way to honor that because if and when you truly love another, you want to find a way to honor them and also honor their requests of you. I knew that I wanted to start a new tradition in my life, one of attending to my sorrow and grief. But in the same moment, I wanted to be able to get hold of my mind and my heart and influence the direction back towards life and the beauty it holds and the value it represents when we live fully and in a place of integrity and gentility.

It was difficult but I had to find a way to rewrite my story, my interpretation of the loss, and so I did. I got very quiet and contemplative and it came to me that God's greatest plan for me was to place my grief next to my great gift. He took my mother at a time when he knew I would have only a short window within which to be completely out of my mind with sorrow, the day of the 4th, the day of the 5th and then I would capture myself and do as I did—which was to embrace my breaths and decide to continue to live to honor both of my parents on the 6th, the day of my birth. I also made an intention to adopt firmly the belief that we are fortunate to outlive our parents since it is so horrible and somehow unnatural for parents to lose their child. I found myself thanking God for the plan of sparing my parents the grief of losing a child.

I felt a similar way when I lost my father and when I suffered other losses that grabbed my heart in a mighty way. The desire to live is strong and the desire to die can be just as strong and is, for that reason, very powerful. We have a desire to escape from what is uncomfortable, and grief is as about as uncomfortable as life gets. However, when you are in the worst possible position in your mind and in your heart, there is the greatest opportunity when feeling bottomed-out to then recognize how awfulness *feels* and to embrace it until it just makes you scream for the option to be released from it and to breathe again and feel life. If I hadn't loved so deeply, the pain of loss would not have been so monumental. It is the depth of the agony that tells us how much we value the connection we have to another, and the connection can never be as rich if we don't have a good, solid, clean heart with which to connect and experience the desire to thrive and live in vibrance.

Your Self Talk Script

Sit quietly now and think about who it is in this world that you have loved more than anything else. Envision that the connection between you and them is deep and beautiful and powerful and that it is so fleeting in this life experience that you must let the passion flow freely, and you must be clear and kind and genteel in your relationship to this precious person.

Write your story with them in a way that maximizes every bit of your strength and sit here with that thinking and hold it close.

Breathe and envision all the ways that love offers you a golden opportunity to manage your stress very well.

To view the video: www.drdebcarlin.com

WHEN YOU SAVE YOUR OWN LIFE, YOUR ARE AVAILABLE TO OTHERS

The issue of life and how to live it fully, getting the most from it and not looking at the lives of others and wishing for what they have, is obviously something important to me. I've spent a lot of time thinking about this. But what is perhaps most fascinating is that I have found these same issues are important to just about everyone I talk with routinely. There is nothing here that is foreign to our mind or our heart. We spend our life with others, we compare our *self* to the *self* of others, and we examine our life and how we are doing it with how others are doing theirs. All of this is why competition becomes a part of our experience in our family life, among friends, with neighbors, and in the workplace, especially when we feel like we just don't measure up to our own expectations of our *self* and we don't meet what others expected of us. At those times there are anxiety and fear and depression along with an awkwardness that makes us less available to our own *self* and also to others.

When I have felt really crummy about myself, I've shut myself off because it is too hard to look and see. How many people do you think share that experience? How many people shut themselves off by getting inebriated in one way or another in order to either stop looking or to see their *self* differently?

I think it is why people decide to escape from normal consciousness altogether. I've asked this question of people who drink a lot of alcohol or do drugs of some sort, and the answer is invariably about a desire to kick back, relax, take it easy, but why the introduction of a substance to do this? The answer is always about freeing the mind, letting the mind go to a different place. I find this fascinating because it's not like we cannot get there without chemical assistance. The concept of mind altering by substances is one that actually isolates us from others. It changes the ability we have to connect in a genuine manner . . . in a manner that allows for the trueness of connection where we meet, as my dear friend, the author Parker Palmer likes to say: deep to deep.

The question is, how do we go deep to deep? What does that mean and why should we even care? My answer is that the experience of life is very deep. If it weren't, there would be no emotion about anything, we'd merely be flat-lined for the entire experience, but that's not how it happens. We do go deep and we get close to one another and we get injured, and we feel the full range of emotions that accompany the thoughts that take us on those emotional journeys. Worse yet, we get tired of our emotions and go through periods of time when we commit to turning them off and adopting the frame of mind that we're not going to risk getting hurt again. I've never met a person yet who has not run through this line of thinking—and acted on it!

Even when there is a catastrophe in a birth and that little person is ill or somehow badly compromised, all of us are born with a multitude of blessings. I have witnessed very badly deformed infants whose mere presence brought forth a compassion from not only those close to them but to humanity overall. I think of a childhood friend of mine, Craig Hall, who became a surgeon who dedicated his life to repairing the well-being of deformed children as a charitable effort because of how it touched his heart. His behavior touched many and created a series of blessings that would have never taken place if those innocent little babies had not been brought into the world in healthy condition.

I think of Stephen Hawking and the ways in which his condition of health has isolated him into a type of isolation that has been a blessing to the world with the energy that has poured forth from his genius brain. Had he been brought into the world in any other form, his life, impact, and purpose would have shifted in some way—and the blessings of him may have never been realized.

Once upon a time here in our American culture, giving birth to a baby that had an intellectual disability meant shame and institutional-ization; times have changed, and the mainstreaming of these children has led to a societal shift wherein these special offspring have increased a healthy awareness about human function and also about compas-sion and acceptance. In my work with these populations, I find that even those we consider to be unfortunate have blessings—for me, I am reminded to pay closer attention to what they see that I do not, to feel what they feel that I do not, and to be more sensitive and patient. I think our best talent is our ability to connect, both to the self and to another. There is an old saying we've all heard: you must love yourself before you can love another. Every being that we encounter offers a chance for a deep connection—back to our self and to that other.

Yes.

It is true because we must first know how it feels inside of our own *self* to receive tender and genuine appreciation before we can know how to offer it to another. We are not mechanical beings; we are deeply feeling, deeply thinking bodies of energy and spirit and complexity. We have ask the question openly and inside of our own mind—what is life all about and what is my purpose here?

To answer this you can spend an entire lifetime of doing nothing else other than contemplating, and there are people who do exactly that. We call them philosophers and religious clergy, and sometimes they are poets. Even if we do not dedicate our public life to answering the question, we ask it privately, and we strive for clarity in the answer—clarity that will guide us to feeling our purpose. That purpose however is shallow without our connection to another. We need one another in order to survive and to thrive, and that means we need to understand human nature so that we can best maneuver our way with the many others we will experience in this life journey—including our own *self*.

Maya Angelou is one of the authors whose writings I really enjoy. She is both tender and tough. One of the things I credit her with articulating so very well is the following: *I've learned that people will forget what you said, people will forget what you did, but people will never forget how you made them feel.* True.

Who is it, in your private life, your personal life, who makes you laugh really hard?

Who brings you to a complete boiling point of anger?

Who prompts you to cry like a baby?

Do you remember exactly what they did or said? Not often, . . . no. We can hold on to grudges and also delightful connections for an entire lifetime and recall only one thing clearly—how that person made us feel.

When we are at our lowest point of feeling, we are actually at a time of prime opportunity. Some call the experience of a complete failure the perfect storm for a great comeback. I agree, but you have to believe it and embrace it. So how does it happen, and do you need to sink before you can benefit from the potential opportunity for a renewed life experience and great availability to another? No. However, what we must each do is become available to our *self* once we have made the commitment to save our life, and when I say "save our life" I mean it in a variety of ways, because there are many ways in which this happens. It can happen for you as it did for me, in the story I related about losing my mother. That, by the way, was only one story. I have saved my life several times.

This means I have worked to recapture my life and to feel the desire to thrive, and in the experiences I have had in this life, which have taken me across that threshold of deep despair more than once—with illness, with loss, with sheer terror and grief, I know I am not unique. All of this is part of the human experience; you just have to touch it and acknowledge it. We have all had our episodes. Some people go through a massive transformation when they have a life-threatening accident or illness. Suddenly everything becomes more precious because of the threat of running out of time here and having death knock on the door. Sometimes it is when we are so sad and heartbroken about a situation that it feels too painful to take the next breath, and we simply want to evaporate from this life so that we feel no more—no more pain, no more anything. These are obvious, overt, magnified scenarios, but there are other more subtle situations that cause people to change their lives.

For some people, the experience of having an opportunity to save their own life is tied to the work they do daily to earn a living. They hate it and look forward every Monday to the nearest Friday so that they can have the weekend to recover from the experience. They feel this week after week and then for months and years, looking forward only to assigned vacation times for escape and eventually counting the days until retirement. What a way to experience life and spend each day.

It is no surprise that statistics indicate very vividly that Monday morning is the most dominant day and time of day for heart attacks. The mind and the body are one. We simply cannot afford to be so unavailable to our self that we ignore the heart's desires and what the mind wants, what it craves. We are called to pay close attention to our *self* and our need for fulfillment and pleasure, and when we do this, we are available not only to our own *self* but we are free to connect with, and be of deep value to, another.

Have you ever had the experience of dating a person who was so self-absorbed that it made you feel insignificant? I had a friend who I initially really enjoyed, at least to the point of wanting to explore that relationship. He was smart and really handsome and pretty funny, and we had fun together. We'd take a great walks and talk and laugh. Initially, we met because a friend thought we'd be helpful to one another—we were both in tough place and he thought we'd be good company.

When we got together we'd talk about our challenges, and initially it seemed like we were sharing—and then, as I reflected, I noticed that I was never saying anything about my life. He had no idea what was going on in my heart and my mind. My talking was in response to his story, his long story, every single day, complaining about his horrible former spouse and all her negative traits and how vile he found her to be. One day I simply asked him, "Do you realize that you are the one who picked her?"

Stunned, he stood there and stared at me with a blank facial expression. I waited for his response. His claim was that she had tricked him. Really? I then took a huge risk and asked, "Are you telling me that you were somehow unaware, that you missed all of her cues and behaviors that you now see? Again, he was stumped. After a few minutes of thinking about it, he told me that in the beginning of any relationship, it feels good to be with another person and you're just happy, so you don't notice those things. I waited and thought for a minute and asked him, "So, you were with her because it was the feelings of happiness that were only available to you when you were with another and not when you were with your own *self*? Now he was truly stuck because he needed to go deep inside of his heart if he were going to answer that question.

During this time, I was being very kind and soft. I really wanted to know. I was not playing a game of harshness, but I was curious as to whether or not he could go deep and look at himself. He told me, very sadly, "Yes, I hate being alone. I hate where my mind drifts off to, and I'd rather be anywhere than with just with myself." I could not help but tear up. This was so heartbreaking to hear, but I had heard this from so many people across the years.

As we sat together, I asked him, "If you cannot be with you, what is it that happens when you are with another? Do you think that you are really available for the other person to know you, to see you, to feel who you are if you are deflecting every bit of yourself? How often do you have the kind of conversation with another that we are having here right now? When was the last time you looked into the eyes of another deeply and with an openness to not just see inside of them but also share what is viewable inside of you?" He could not remember.

I then asked him, "How available are you to your own *self*? How will you feel if today is your last day of being alive and you die alone? Will you be available to you own *self* enough to experience your exit embracing how full your life was? Or will you be in complete agony with regret and anger that you failed here and had a lonesome and unsatisfying journey?"

He cried, and so did I. And in that moment, I gave him the most enormous and loving hug I have ever extended to another, and I thanked him for being available enough to himself to be available to me. We sat together for many hours, talking deep to deep. He looked at his *self*, and he allowed me to talk to him about the reality that whatever is inside of our *self* is not scary. It is who we are and it needs tending to, by us, not by others, but by us more than by others, forever. When we do allow others in, they need to be ready to give more to us than just something we feel is a void being filled. Because if we don't tend to us, and we expect another to fill every need, even the ones we can fill, every relationship is doomed for failure through disappointment.

We became very good friends after that episode, and he took a number of steps to learn about going deep and learning to love his *self*. This was a man who had his first heart attack when he was barely 40, had another at 44, another at 47, and had gone through women and relationships like they meant nothing all because he was cut off from his own self and didn't take the opportunity to save his own life. Each woman he met and found an interest in quickly became a physically intimate partner, but not really intimate in a healthy emotional way, just physically useful. He had physical closeness by proximity, not through any genuine connection. These encounters gave him brief satisfaction quickly followed by lonesome feelings.

With this turning-point experience, however, he opened and took many positive steps to become open to his *self* and open to the idea that he needed to save his own life. He is now a decade beyond that day and has had no heart attacks, no health issues, and is happily married. His wife adores him because of the good and true person he is, and it works because they are available to one another in every genuine sense.

The question for you now is, how available are you . . . to your own *self*?

Do you know who the best and the deepest parts of you are? How do you get there?

Your Self Talk Script

I invite you, right now, to sit quietly. Open your mind to knowing who the you of the *self* is. Know this as your starting point—we were all created from a source, a source that has created a magnificent universe. Regardless of your religious beliefs, you have nothing to lose by thinking and embracing the idea of magnificent source. When a source creates such beauty, how evil can it possibly be?

We are from it, we are one with it, and we are form one another. We are all connected to each other for better and for worse. We are just simply people. Why not explore what the person is that is you?

Think of who you are, in simple terms: not your job, but your basic character. Look for what is of value and what is most precious and beauty filled, and hold that in your mind right now.

Come back to this place each day and at some point during each day when you think you can give yourself five minutes to say hello to your soul and become available to you. You'll be amazed at what is going to happen.

To view the video: www.drdebcarlin.com

Journaling Exercise

Privately . . . just here for you . . .
reveal in your own script what exactly motivated you
toward this work . . .

Why is this important for you?

If you have the power, what will the outcome of this work
for you produce?

STRESS AND YOUR BEAUTIFUL BODY

There is so much for us to learn in this life experience, and the idea of how best to take care of our body is somehow not high on the list, at least not in most cultures, and certainly not in America. We eat to make our mouth happy and to fill our belly. Few people know their anatomy and fewer understand their own physiology. In America we run to a physician to answer our curious questions about what is taking place within our body, and we are often frustrated because doctors don't seem to have all of the answers. Unfortunately, many times they cannot provide right answers because we don't even know how to accurately and reliably report the questions, but most people don't factor that reality into the equation.

There is a simple solution, and the beauty is that it is never too late for us to study our body and learn the important ways in which our mind and body are so very interconnected. They influence one another with every breath, every thought, and every emotion. It's fascinating.

I think it is kind of funny, although it should not be a laughable matter, that we don't know our body. Why is that?

When we are infants, we are very busy placing our hand into our mouth and even a foot! But as time goes on, we divorce our *self* from knowing who we are. Some of this is because we're told not to play with our *self* in toddlerhood when we start exploring our genitals and parents don't want us to get obsessed or embarrass them in public, but that is only a small aspect of the challenges we face. We just don't know our bodies.

Do you know where your gallbladder is? And which connects to your stomach—the small or the large intestine? Do your tonsils serve any purpose? What does it mean if you have high blood pressure or high cholesterol? And why should you care?

If you are thinking that this is silly because you have a doctor who tends to all of that for you and you have drugs and medicines to help you, I invite you to consider rethinking your outlook and here is why.

Taking medicine does not guarantee that you won't suffer from the consequences of the thing you are taking the medicine for or that you won't have additional problems because of the medicine; we all know about side effects. Additionally, physicians need for us to let them know us when we feel well in addition to when we're under the weather or injured. They need to know our emotional state, our belief system, who we are, and what our life expectations are. And if you think I am kidding, test it out.

Physicians went into their careers with a list of needs and one was to help people. There is no way to be of real help if you don't understand who these people are. Simple truth. I cannot possibly make decisions for you in good conscience that are aligned with your lifestyle if I don't understand who you are. What happens when patients and physicians don't know one another is called "compliance issues." There is a breakdown in what the doctor tells you to do and what you actually do. In my experience, that happens because the two parties don't really know one another *and* the patient does not fully understand his or her own body enough to appreciate the implications of the request/recommendation/prescription.

I recently met a young woman who had lived with the problem of stomach ulcers—bleeding ulcers, which were a terrible problem. Her doctor prescribed various medications and finally surgery, a surgery which ended up in the removal of her stomach. I was horrified. These doctors were looking to find relief for her but they didn't know her, and they didn't know her lifestyle and her desires for a full and rich existence beyond that surgery. And she did not understand the implications of having such a dramatic procedure done. She was unaware of the role of the stomach in the body overall, let alone the role it plays in the digestive system. Now that she is experiencing kidney failure, I am eagerly in search of ways to educate her and get her familiar enough with her body so she can contribute in meaningful ways to help a professional team understand more productively what she is experiencing, so that treatments are not created from a text book that doesn't take her uniqueness into account.

Had this young woman understood the mind–body connection and the genuine influence that our thoughts and emotions have over our physiology, in addition to what foods could be very healing and healthy for an ulcerative condition, she might have been spared her current situation.

What do I mean by that . . . ? . . . !

For every thought we have, there is an emotion associated and vice versa. These pairings release neurotransmitters into our blood stream and cause our body to do *things*. What sorts of things? There are many examples, but let's continue with the stomach example. When your stomach churns and burns, it isn't necessarily due to something you ate; the stomach is a typical place for stress to manifest itself. Discomfort in the stomach more likely stems from some aggravation, some stress you've been experiencing, and this happens because as you stress out, you are swallowing air and also producing digestive juices as you salivate which trigger digestive juices to be released into your digestive system. When there is no food or insufficient food to absorb those secretions, your gut literally gets attacked.

The feeling of being queasy, having the feeling of fullness even if you've not eaten, and having bloating, abdominal gas, and stomach upsets are some of the first symptoms of stress. In addition to the stomach's involvement, the large intestine is where most of the action takes place. Food stays in your stomach for just 30 minutes, but it can take 48 to 72 hours for partially digested particles to work through the entire length of the large intestine. The presence of stress hormones slows digestion further, so when you're under pressure, food can ferment and stagnate, leading to diarrhea and constipation. These activities combined shift the live flora in the digestive tract, which is what keeps it healthy and also helps break down food. If you don't tend to the stress and these physical reactions through specific dietary aids like aloe juice or live yogurt which replenish and minimize the reactions, you run the risk of creating a breakdown in the lining of your gut and end up producing sores which are ulcerative. If this sounds complex to you, please believe me that it is only because of the initial exposure you're having to these concepts here. It is actually very simple.

Here is the simplicity: our mind and body and very tied together, and by more than just the neck. Our heart and our brain travel everywhere with us and they follow one another. When we have thoughts and feelings, we need to embrace them and own them, and deal with the consequences, not try to escape them—not any portion of them. I'm not being frivolous when I state overtly that we each need to take much more gentle and loving care of our mind and our body, and work to understand both.

Authors like the popular Dr. Oz have written books like *The Owner's Manual*. There are vast resources available to us all online. Libraries are filled with resources. Study *you*—find out what your body is doing; the rewards are high and when you understand your body, you become less afraid of your symptoms because you understand them. Once you understand them, you know how to either treat them yourself or explain in a helpful manner to a professional what's happening so they can assist you more effectively.

I know for example, that if I am craving coffee in the morning, I need to eat yogurt first. Otherwise I have two reactions to coffee on an empty gut: a stomachache because the acid is burning my raw gut lining and anxiety because I am absorbing caffeine at too rapid a rate without food to digest and absorb some of it. My having a morning coffee without this knowledge can me feel like I am going insane and dying simultaneously.

The other part of the understanding our body mind connection is to acknowledge that we each know full well why our body looks the way it does. Ok, this is big for me—because this is my personal story.

I grew up athletic and slender. Now is a different story and a different body. I could tell myself stories about how it is because I am older and I have slowed my pace or my metabolism is slower or some other halfway plausible nonsense, but I know the real deal, the real perspective. Here it is. I am pretty chunky. There is nothing I can do on the camera here to hide that fact—this is me. Many days I just say "yikes."

A decade ago I was pretty good looking, but when I lost my husband, it really broke my heart, I mean to the core. It was a loss, a major hit to my soul, the very core of me. I was initially so grief-stricken that I did not self-nourish and I lost quite a bit of weight from being a normal-weight person. People thought I looked great. Really? I thought they were nuts because I felt awful, but in our culture, thin is in. It is gorgeous even if you are depressed. Suddenly, I found myself attracting men, and I was in no way ready for that—not at all. I recoiled and isolated myself, and I stayed at home and ate whatever I wanted. It is a very easy formula. Trust me, if you don't know this routine, chances are you will some day, or you will certainly know someone who does this or has done this. I gained maybe 30 or 40 pounds and didn't have to worry about handsome men desiring my intimate companionship. I was relieved.

I went from that into my work and that was even easier because there was none of that sexual tension with anyone in my career world. I was free. My work thrived. I was increasingly more effective. Interesting. It felt to me like everyone was more relaxed around me.

The problem was I kept eating whatever I wanted and not worrying about weight or exercise. I'd been pretty healthy.

Then . . . well, in the last section you heard my story about my mom—all very true. I turned off my business and redirected my life. I wanted to do nothing other than sit next to my mom and tend to her and enjoy whatever time we had together, to savor it, and she'd either get well, and we'd get healthy together or something else would occur.

The "something else" occurred. She passed away. I got really sad all over again and her message to me for months before she had died was: Deb, please be happy again, I want you to have a full life when I am gone. What is happening here is no way to live. Get healthy; fall in love again. I would look at her and remind her we were on this path together and all things would come to pass as was our fates.

When my mom died, I was pretty chunked out, in another state of grief. I sure didn't feel like eating, so weight dropped off a bit. Then I had to replay in my mind my mom's requests of me to be healthy, to be happy. Those thoughts gave me a very physical response and began to generate inside of me a desire to love life.

I am giving you the short version here, but it was very difficult—hard to come to terms with—the idea of going on with my life. I found myself wondering what my purpose was, what my intent was, what my gifts and skills were. Grief does that to you, and your body attends to that. I got into some real trouble as a result of my sadness and despair just as with stress. My joints began to hurt, movement became a challenge, weight sat on my frame, I felt tired all of the time, and I had some enormous dental problems—awful, just awful, and it is all inter-related.

Guess what?! It is now two years later. I've dropped several sizes in my clothing, I swim nearly every day, I crave healthy foods, I have taken care of my dental health, and have my beautiful mouth again. I can move more freely and without pain or agony most of the time (still working on this) and my energy is resuming. I've changed my state physiologically and it has altered my story psychologically or vice versa; they work together. The point is, when I decided to take my next breath, to rejoin the living, to pursue a really great life once again, my mind and my body began to work together in a new direction once again—they shift gears easily!

Now, as I envision myself alive and vibrant, I also envision spectacular men to date and simply play with and maybe even fall in love with, and as a result of that freeing, I drop excess weight. I also swim and eat in a healthy way. I am not on a rigid diet of some artificial routine. I am on a steady diet of I love life!

Your Self Talk Script

I begin each morning as I invite you to do here. Look up at the sky or out the window, search to see something beautiful in nature. Give thanks, truly, for your ability to see and also to hear the rustlings of leaves, the break of the waters, the songs of the birds, the wind moving the leaves on the trees. Whatever source you believe in, gives thanks, now. I do and I also say that I am thankful for the ability to breath each day. I do not live on a ventilator as I have seen too many do. I can move. I am not restrained in any way. I am so thank-filled, and I can think clearly; my mind works reliably for me. My heart is open, open to love, and open to possibilities. It is a new day, it is a fresh breath, it is life, this is life. I want to have passion and feel it and embrace it, every bit of it ,and be thankful for every aspect of it, because it causes me to be inspired and motivated and do good works for the people around me and for the people of the planet.

I am blessed and happy and at peace. My body is what is me and I love me. And because of my mind and my thoughts, I am ready to love my body completely and to enjoy and embrace my health and to cherish and protect my health with everything I do to and with and for my body, every day.

Retain this line of thinking here and practice it daily.

To view the video: www.drdebcarlin.com

What You Put in Your Mouth and Why It Really Matters

By now perhaps you have noticed that I happen to think that "funny" is really good. Life is funny, isn't it? Not always in the ways we would like but somehow entertaining. My dad used to tell me that things in life are always funny, just not always funny-ha-ha, just sometimes funny, interesting, or odd. He was right—right just about all of the time—bless his heart.

What's so funny about the topic here today, for this episode, about what you put into your mouth? Well, several things.

First off, you have to know that nothing ever happens in isolation, not really.

Our health and happiness and well-being is about a whole lot more than just the food we place into our mouth, it is also about everything we imbibe, smoke, and it is about what we do with other people. Yes, whether you are talking about kissing or going way beyond that. Who we kiss and become invested in is every bit a component of our diet as food is. It can help us be more healthy or be completely crazy.

My mom and dad both took time to talk to me when I was a child and then also an adolescent, even when I didn't want them giving me their input. I had to listen though even when I didn't want to pay attention. Their messaging to me penetrated and is alive within me to this day, decades later, threaded through my professional training and experience and wrapped around my personal life trials and tribulations.

The core of their message to me was about valuing the self. Their message was to always value your *self*, place a high value on who you are. This included how you talk to your own *self*, how you present your *self* to the world, how you interact with others, and how you allow others to treat you. Although this sounds very basic and simple, the follow-through on it behaviorally is very tough, especially if you are not used to being so conscious and considerate of who you are. They also told me to be very conscious about my mouth—not just what I ate and how politely I consumed food, but also how I spoke: they told be to be careful about my words and my tone of voice and my facial gestures as well. They really encouraged me to be conscious of these behaviors.

My parents gave me this messaging to the point of telling me not to date or kiss just anyone, but to be discerning and to make conscious choices. Great advice. And to take it a few steps further, they told me not to select a mate without that same degree of contemplation. So many people end up in a split in their marriage or love affairs and even friendships and working partnerships because they didn't really honor who they are. In a sense, it was a result of this that they kissed the wrong person and ended up eating bad food and becoming fat and unhealthy in some regard. It all ties together. We don't enter onto a path of unhealthy self-destruction when we're happy with our self and our partner.

When we make thoughtless selections about anything in this life, we are committing a form of slow and indirect suicide. This happens when we eat for our mouth instead of our overall body and state of health. I'm a real expert at this. I love oral satisfaction; imbibing and eating are favorite past times of mine and always have been. And here in America, just like everywhere else around the globe, we hold our life celebrations around food and drink.

Think of every holiday, every special occasion. People want to get together and eat. I can sit here now and tell you the traditional family menus I grew up on for every holiday, and you can do same. When I worked in cardiac rehab units as the visiting psychologist, I would talk to the patients while they were on their treadmills and cycles and ask them how they landed up with a heart event. They invariably told me it was in their genes. I listened. I'd hear about the parents and grandparents and how they had similar issues and how someone in their lineage had a similar challenge with their health.

After hearing the stories, I would transition the conversations into having them tell me how they spent their holidays. I'd have them share their favorite dishes and describe vividly what Thanksgiving and Christmas or Hanukkah looked like at their house when they were growing up. And now, and most of the time, they were dutifully maintaining their lineage with these menus and prized recipes, and I did the same. We also talked about the ways they had spent their life in movement or in stillness, such as out in the farm fields or behind a desk, taking walks for errands, or getting into a car for every little thing.

What became apparent was that for most of these people, the trends of the style with which they lived their life was a clear repeat of the habits they had learned from family. No harm or blame is meant here, but it is just a simple reality, and as a result their reality also included the pathway in regard to health that their ancestors had experienced. Instead of thinking about this course of theirs in terms of a fate due to genetics, I invited them to just contemplate the ways in which there was a different factor at work.

In social psychology this is the impact of role modeling on an individual, the copying of the behaviors we observe, consciously and unconsciously, because that process of observation is powerful, very deeply powerful. In fact, it is so powerful that grown people will get angry, frustrated, tearful, and resentful if and when you take away from them their access to those things. They want so much to have role models across their lifetime, that it can place them into a dangerous and untenable position with certain of their healthcare workers who occasionally pressure them to make lifestyle changes that put them at risk of jeopardizing their health.

Why are our lifestyle changes so tough to make?

The toughness of making healthy changes is all about our attitudes and perceptions. Food is a reward for us. What we place into our mouth is done more for pleasure than for substantial need. I don't need to have an ice cream sundae, but on a day of celebration, I want to bring forward my pleasant memories from the past and engage in those activities that produce pleasure—there's nothing wrong with that except doing it too frequently in too many situations where we check out of our state of awareness to enter a place of indulgence. This is a part of the human condition. Some people call it gluttony, others label it sin, some say it is addiction, and others will claim it is about free will. Probably each explanation has some percentage of accuracy. The point, however, is that when we do things that we enjoy, that are special and precious, we simply need awareness to be "present" about what the implications of our actions are.

When it comes to food, our body needs good fuel in order to operate at a level where we can sustain performance. At what level of performance do you want to be?

When we think of what we imbibe, whether we drink alcohol, tea, coffee, water, or something else, the correct thought process needs to be present so that we are aware of what this fuel is doing to our physiology. I have mentioned the reality that too often we are unaware of our own anatomy and physiology. Now is a great time to become increasingly more curious about the impact of any of these liquids upon your *self.*

Sound silly? If it does, come in a little closer. Try an experiment with yourself: imbibe none or a large quantity of something and pay close attention to the effects. For me, a pot of coffee can become a nightmare—psychologically and digestively—remember my sharing that story? Alcohol is another. A glass of wine is fun as a celebratory gesture or to complement a food experience, but this experience is short-lived since it also creates a drowsy sensation that places me into an early slumber, and as a result, I now only drink alcohol on rare occasions. It used to be fun, but my awareness of the consequences has shifted. I want to be in the moment and be highly conscious and aware of every single thing.

Over these years of my life, I have felt a certain empowerment in coming to the realization that everything I place into my mouth is in my absolute control. I cannot put the blame on anyone else for my weight or for my physiological state, a fact that is both psychologically sickening and also freeing. Since I have come into the space in my living experience of wanting to really thrive, really live well, and become my very best, I am finding my cravings, my choices, and my intentions have shifted into a gear I find really satisfying. And I mean that with food and drink and also with the kissing theme.

How many people have gone out on the weekend, had too much liquor, hooked up with someone, and had crazy kissing and even more intimate sex? That's all about why what you put into your mouth at every level is so important. Stop for a moment and consider how many people are in rehab units. It is all about what they began putting into their mouth and then maybe up their nose or into their veins. Look at people who smoke nicotine and need to cough their throats dry to clear their lungs form the junk that smoking produces in them. Look at the people who have health issues that have caused them to become hypertensive and to have heart attacks, strokes, and diabetes. So much of it is a result of their lifestyle, their habits, and their choices. Where was their strength within to guide them and help them? In truth, it was right there, deep within them, but they turned the other way.

This entire series, all of my work and intentionality, is about not turning the other way. Friends, listen . . . listen closely to what your mind tells you when you turn up the intuitive voice, the voice I told you about earlier. If you've forgotten, turn back and review it again because it is critical for you and for your life. There is just one experience here, this life experience. I don't know what happens after all of this. Do we come back again? Do we go to heaven or burn in hell or are we just gone? No one *really* knows. I have faith and beliefs, but no solid assurance, no policy written someplace, but what I do know is that I was created as a complete human being and I have strength within me that I tap into and it brings me results that are vibrant and healthy when I allow it.

I'm not interested in giving into momentary pleasures with my mouth here, my fabulous mouth, only to pay penalties later that can literally cost me my life. So the food that goes through this passageway is most often healthy and great fuel. The liquids are, too, and it's really fun to explore new healthy foods and drinks. The choices are seemingly endless, and they are delicious and nutritious, just good for you with no junk like nicotine and certainly no kissing of frogs. I love everything that I am being discerning about, and it is not about deprivation. It is about smart choices that will enhance my life, not compromise it.

Your Self Talk Script

Envision what our deepest strength is when we focus on this beautiful mouth . . . that sits right here on the front of our face to greet the world and invite into us what is good and pure and splendid, and that is what we want because we crave wellness, health, and beauty and being alive to breathe in the air and feel strong. We can achieve every bit of this because we are in control of this aspect of our life experience. We can say what we want to select because we are in control of our mind and of our thoughts. We can place good things into our mouth that will add to our strength and enjoyment in this life experience . . . yes, say yes. Say yes to being conscious and aware and awake. Envision every part of you being that way, and allow the strength within you to emerge.

To view the video: www.drdebcarlin.com

MOVEMENT, ALIGNMENT & FREEDOM

How does your body feel when you first awaken in the morning? Do you spring up into action or do you take a bit of time to get oriented? Do you emerge knowing the challenges you will have from the moment you put your feet on the ground, hoping your knees and hips and back will sustain you?

National statistics in America reveal that too many of us are arising to pain, impaired movement, and to generally being out of whack. What a way to start the day. What is it that such a reality does to us as we awaken and approach life once again?

You may notice in this series that I am not here as a perfect specimen of how to live 100 percent in the realm of being conscious and aware and awake. In fact, it has been the many experiences of my lack of paying attention, or even not caring, or of just exercising poor judgment that resulted in the experience of my awakenings and re-awakenings. From that comes my desire, and my passion to share what I have learned from my own life and from others about what works well to produce a great life. I am certainly on my pathway of not just having a good life, but having an ever increasingly better, richer, happier, healthier life.

If we are each to know the strength that lies within us, we need to feel that strength, and unless there is something unusual and catastrophic, we need the experience to extend into our physical realm. We are physical beings. When I am saying "something unusual or catastrophic," I mean events like the kind of challenges that Stephen Hawking has or that the much admired Christopher Reeves, had after his equestrian accident.

As babies, we have such flexibility. Have you ever just sat and watched a baby as they pull their foot into their mouth? They are so bendy. Little children can stretch and flex and move and jump and twirl and run and it seems so effortless. Do you remember that?

Are you still child-like in your ability to move?

I'm not, and it is one big fat journey to resume and regain that element of movement and alignment that I took for granted when I was young. We always take our freedoms for granted, or so I observe.

Although we can each produce a story about the "why" behind whatever it is that has contributed to our aging of our body, the facts are clear. You either move it or you lose it. And just as we have the pairing of a thought and emotion that releases chemicals into our body to cause us to feel and react, our emotions and our body's experience of the reactions to these emotions travel through our body and can land in interesting places that cause us to experience stiffness and aches and even agony. People who do massage therapy, chiropractics, and acupuncture or physical therapy, can all tell where it is that you place and store stress in your body. Additionally, they can tell you how much stress you've been experiencing because of the manner in which your body does or does not move and align. This is interesting and very valuable.

If you dive into this topic, you will be amazed to discover how much your body has shifted to accommodate your emotions.

I know for my own well-being that I have to move and get into a high gear each day when I first arise or else my body will be very stiff, and my joints, especially my knees, will complain to me all day long. A result of that agony will diminish my energy and render me less productive, and that will create a vicious cycle of frustration and stressfulness. Upon awakening, I either go for a brisk walk or I go for a lap swim. I need to get my state of physiology in gear alongside my mind because, as you recall, we have to respect that the mind and body go everywhere together.

Pete Egoscue is the author of a series about living pain-free. He is a highly renowned physical therapist who took his professional experience to great heights by paying close attention to what he observed and applied it to what he knew intuitively would make a difference. Living with pain robs you of the strength that is yours to embrace and utilize to have a meaningful and impactful life. Living with pain when you rely on pharmaceuticals of any sort to deal with the pain is just pretending to have a solution. It is pretending because unless those substances are curing you, they are merely masking the pain, and the pain is actually helpful as an indicator of what you need to attend to.

Pete's methods are all about alignment, and his theory makes great sense. Basically, if one part of you is out of alignment, the rest of you gets out of alignment as well. Over time, everything is a bit crooked and pain is your new companion. I invite you to Google Pete's name and read up on his techniques. Some of what might be an issue for you can be solved through his readings that are completed with excellent illustrations.

In addition to swimming and walking, I know I have to do physical exercises that will compensate for the many hours I spend being still while I work at my desk. I spend hours each day on the phone or writing. I love my desk and my office and my chair, but I don't want to end up confined to them. Most days, as important as I like to pretend I am, the world as I know it and as it knows me can function just fine while I take a few hours for myself for an afternoon break of sunshine and play time, all year round. I invite you to do the same.

When I feel myself moving freely without restriction, I feel nearly invincible and certainly feel my strength. And that generalizes over into my intellectual and emotional capabilities and influences my beliefs about what I can do in any dimension of my life.

I recently went to a very special meeting where I got to see, meet, talk to, and be in the absolutely delightful and fascinating presence of the author Tony Robbins—a fascinating man. He tells his story of his life and how he discovered time and again his inner strength. He inspired me. A friend of mine had commented to me before that journey to see Tony Robbins that he knew I would return in another level of an enlightened state and believing in myself, even though the meeting was about mastering my business. And my friend was correct. It didn't matter what the topic was: a man like Tony Robbins is not going to invest the time in sharing information if he notices that you don't have the capacity in you to find and tap into your inner strength so that you can really and truly do *it*, whatever *it* is. Lots of people dream; in fact, all people dream, but only some of the people actually enable their dreams and see them come true. Why is that?

One reason for this I consistently observe is that people just sit and pretend and then write the wrong story about why they could not make their dreams a reality. I hear many excuses. However, when people are living pain-free, are up and moving and feeling their body, and feeling their ability to experience the richness of life through their physical dimension, they are stronger, more vibrant, and more productive in every way.

So what is the formula here? Self talk can establish that inner belief, that new story that begins right here and now with your next breath.

Your Self Talk Script

Be here now. Pay close attention . . . to you . . . See yourself in your best physical shape in your mind's eye right now! See it and hold it there and know that it is there because of what you have done with you mind—your mind has directed your body to move and to be healthy through good choices, great judgments, and ongoing healthy habits. You do all of these things because you crave being vibrant and powerful.

You are gorgeous because you are moving freely, and with every movement, you come to know more deeply how good you are at doing whatever it is that you set your mind to do . . . and it is enormous. You can walk, you can swim, you can jump, and you can run. It just takes times, a plan, and a strategy to make it happen . . . but you can make anything you want happen.

Keep these words in your mind's eye. Think them, believe them, embrace them, let them penetrate your mind and your body . . . keep your *self* talk affirming and loving. Keep your *self* aware and compassion filled.

To view the video: www.drdebcarlin.com

SELF-ASSESSMENT
Mind & Body Integration

Understanding the connections between mind and body is both intuitive and also considered to be a type of intelligence equally as crucial as your IQ or your emotional intelligence or social intelligence. Intelligence and intuition work together to create an awareness for us so we can interpret bodily sensations. The sensations we experience provide feedback and guidance about every facet of our functioning and our reactions to our life on a daily and even on a moment-to-moment basis.

The opening question for you here is: how intuitive and intelligently tuned into your own self are you when it comes to the connection between your mind and your body? Think carefully, and reply to the questions.

Answer honestly. If you don't, then this is just a silly game that is a waste of time—especially yours.

1 = not at all   9 = all the way

1. I have a clear understanding of my anatomy and physiology.

    1   2   3   4   5   6   7   8   9

2. I am comfortable in my own body and can interpret signs and symptoms.

    1   2   3   4   5   6   7   8   9

3. I know how to manage my signs and symptoms.

    1   2   3   4   5   6   7   8   9

4. I believe it my physician's job to know my body and manage my signs and symptoms.

    1   2   3   4   5   6   7   8   9

5. Emotions have no impact upon my anatomy and physiology.

    1   2   3   4   5   6   7   8   9

6. My personal thoughts have no impact upon my anatomy and physiology.

    1   2   3   4   5   6   7   8   9

7. My social interactions have no impact upon my anatomy and physiology.

    1   2   3   4   5   6   7   8   9

8. Illness is the result of forces external to me and my control—like genetics, infections, and luck.

    1   2   3   4   5   6   7   8   9

9. Recovery from illness is dependent upon who your physician is.

    1   2   3   4   5   6   7   8   9

List your continual symptoms, if any:

PLAN OF ACTION TOOL
Resolution Reflections

When we understand the concepts of the mind and body connection, and give it the merit needed, we gain power because we gain the ability to influence our mind and the manner in which our body reacts. The mind is the only thing in this life we can control. And our mind has tremendous control over our body.

The Biopsychosocial model description and it's application in medicine

The biological component of the model seeks to understand how the cause of the illness stems from the functioning of the individual's body. The psychological component looks for psychological causes for a health problem. The social part of the model seeks the social issues that influence health.

The biopsychosocial model of health is based, in part, on social cognitive theory. The biopsychosocial model implies that treatment of disease processes requires the healthcare team to address biological, psychological, and social influences on a functioning and healthy individual. The biopsychosocial model states that the workings of the body affect the mind, and the workings of the mind affect the body. There is both a direct interaction between mind and body as well as indirect effects through intermediate factors.

The biopsychosocial model presumes it is important to handle physical, mental, and social realities. Empirical literature suggests that patient perceptions of health and the threat of disease, as well as barriers in the social or cultural environment, appear to influence the likelihood that a person will engage in promoting their health with a proper diet, good nutrition and engaging in physical activity, or will recoil from this and behave in counterproductive ways.

Your plan of action includes the following 3-Step Plan. Even if you are a healthcare professional, there is merit in taking another look to get a fresh perspective

A 3-Step Plan

1. Obtain a copy of each of the following five:

    The Mindbody Prescription:
    Healing the Body, Healing the Pain
    by John E. Sarno, MD

    Minding the Body, Mending the Mind
    by Joan Borysenko, PhD

    The Relaxation Response
    by Miriam Z. Klipper & Herbert Benson, MD

    The Mind's Eye
    by Deborah Carlin, PhD

    YOU: The Owner's Manual, Updated and Expanded Edition:
    An Insider's Guide to the Body that Will Make You
    Healthier and Younger
    by Mehmet C. Oz, MD and Michael F. Roizen, MD

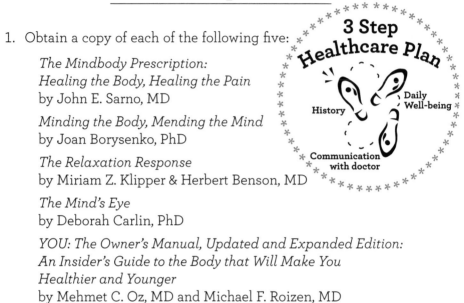

2. Take daily notes on your emotions and your symptoms. Place them into your day planner so you can take them and see if there are patterns that emerge in relation to schedule, diet, activities, time of month, or other factors.

3. Make an appointment with your internist, share the information, and create an open rapport.

Additional Important Steps

Write here what your dialogue with your physician will entail.

What questions do you have?

What do you want to say?

What is important to you that your primary physician needs to understand about you? Remember, and believe, it is in knowing you that someone can really care for you.

Be sure to include conversation about your Advance Directives (do you have them?) Visit www.DrDebCarlin.com for a template.

Do you have a long-term care policy in place so that you can direct the care you receive if you need to and also decide where you will receive it and by whom? Be sure you have a policy with the options that are important to you.

What would you like such a plan to include? Once you know this, you can make sure you have it in place.

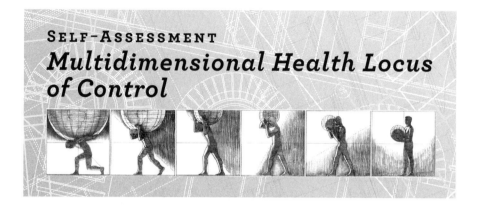

SELF-ASSESSMENT
Multidimensional Health Locus of Control

Instructions: Each item below is a belief statement about your medical condition about which you may agree or disagree. Beside each statement is a scale that ranges from strongly disagree (1) to strongly agree (6). For each item circle the number that represents the extent to which you agree or disagree with that statement. The more you agree with a statement, the higher the number should be that you choose to circle. The more you disagree with a statement, the lower the number should be that you choose to circle. Please make sure that you answer **EVERY ITEM** and that you circle **ONLY ONE** number per item. This is a measure of your personal beliefs. Obviously, there are no right or wrong answers.

		SD	MD	D	A	MA	SA
1=Strongly Disagree (SD) 2=Moderately Disagree (MD) 3=Slightly Disagree (D)	4=Slightly Agree (A) 5=Moderately Agree (MA) 6=Strongly Agree (SA)						
1	If I get sick, it is my own behavior which determines how soon I get well again.	1	2	3	4	5	6
2	No matter what I do, if I am going to get sick, I will get sick.	1	2	3	4	5	6
3	Having regular contact with my physician is the best way for me to avoid illness.	1	2	3	4	5	6
4	Most things that affect my health happen to me by accident.	1	2	3	4	5	6
5	Whenever I don't feel well, I should consult a medically trained professional.	1	2	3	4	5	6
6	I am in control of my health.	1	2	3	4	5	6
7	My family has a lot to do with my becoming sick or staying healthy.	1	2	3	4	5	6
8	When I get sick, I am to blame.	1	2	3	4	5	6
9	Luck plays a big part in determining how soon I will recover from an illness.	1	2	3	4	5	6
10	Health professionals control my health.	1	2	3	4	5	6
11	My good health is largely a matter of good fortune.	1	2	3	4	5	6
12	The main thing which affects my health is what I myself do.	1	2	3	4	5	6
13	If I take care of myself, I can avoid illness.	1	2	3	4	5	6
14	Whenever I recover from an illness, it's usually because other people (for example, doctors, nurses, family, friends) that have been taking good care of me.	1	2	3	4	5	6
15	No matter what I do, I 'm likely to get sick.	1	2	3	4	5	6
16	If it's meant to be, I will stay healthy.	1	2	3	4	5	6
17	If I take the right actions, I can stay healthy.	1	2	3	4	5	6
18	Regarding my health, I can only do what my doctor tells me to do.	1	2	3	4	5	6

Scoring Instructions for the MHLC Scales

SUBSCALE	FORM(s)	POSSIBLE RANGE	ITEMS
Internal	A, B, C	6 - 36	1, 6, 8, 12, 13, 17
Chance	A, B, C	6 - 36	2, 4, 9, 11, 15, 16
Powerful Others	A, B	6 - 36	3, 5, 7, 10, 14, 18
Doctors	C	3 - 18	3, 5, 14
Other People	C	3 - 18	7, 10, 18

I used this instrument in my graduate degree work when conducting my research on hypertension and interventions. The intervention of choice was Herbert Benson's Relaxation Response. Dr. Benson is a world-renowned cardiologist. His work has launched incredibly helpful mind/body research. Google his name and explore his good material. I elected to utilize Dr. Benson's work and also measure the degree to which people's attitudes would shift once they realized they could actually gain not only influence but control over their own physiology. The Wallston's research on internal perceptions about control were very timely. Their generosity to me has now extended to others so that their tools are available in the public domain to all of us.

The scoring gives an indication of your attitudes about your health for you to explore. You need to know where it is that you place control with respect to your health and your health outcomes. You either believe that this is in your control, or you believe the status of your health is just a matter of chance, or you believe the status of your health is controlled by some influential and powerful others like your doctors or other people in your life.

The point is that you need to be aware of your attitudes about the responsibility for your healthcare choices.

PLAN OF ACTION TOOL
Health Control

My invitation for you is to create the following plan of action instead of allowing worries to creep in.

Begin with awareness of the tool and the scoring.

If you have not taken enough responsibility for your health issues, allow yourself to shift your focus from having too much external control of your health decisions to having an internal locus of control, and work to gain the control of the future of your own health.

Practice relaxation daily and allow the assessments you have taken thus far to influence you to take a more potent role in your own destiny.

Write what you are willing to do:

Describe five goals:

Commit to a specific timeline:

Durable Information to Support Your Plan of Action

The idea behind the questionnaire about your health locus of control has a strong academic history. It was Julian Rotter who, in the 1950s, began writing about his curiosity about how people interpreted events in their life and to what degree they could influence them. He developed it into a theory that psychologists, including me, have found fascinating. Using Latin as his format, he began to investigate the psychological location of where a person believed the control of their life came from—either internally or externally. If you have a strong sense that you are in control of your life events, you are said to have an internal locus of control. If you believe that your life is controlled by other forces be it powerful people or God or fate or luck, you are identified as having an external locus of control. There are interesting implications for both positions and, of course, there is a self-assessment to help you determine where you land.

When you are in internal locus of control person, you behave in a manner that is consistent; you tend to be an influencer and proactive. You believe you have a degree of authority that can impact the outcomes you would like to see happen. Those whose control is external to them also behave in manners consistent with that belief and are more prone to be less proactive and to seek out others for guidance, and they are most likely to blame fate or bad luck on outcomes they regret.

Rotter's theory and self-assessment tool are based on a continuum. A person is not typically internal or external to an extreme but falls somewhere in between. Although his theory is fascinating, it is the research it inspired that is really remarkable and of direct application for us with respect to our well-being.

In 1976 Kenneth Wallston was a research psychologist at Vanderbilt University. He was not only interested in Rotter's work, but saw that it could be used to better understand how people behave specifically in relation to their individual health issues. He was right. With his team, he developed the Multidimensional Health Locus of Control Scale—the same one used in this book and program materials. The instrument has such a high level of credibility and validity that it has been used by psychologists and health professionals for decades.

During the time I was in graduate school, I used this for my master's degree thesis research. My interest was in the disturbing prevalence of cardiovascular disease we have in America, the foundation of which is either atherosclerotic disease and/or hypertension. My theory was that if I could teach people who suffer from hypertension how to become normotensive using Herbert Benson's Relaxation Response exercise, they would see the impact they can have on their health and become internal with respect to their locus of control overall and with respect to their health.

The project was a success because, indeed, when people come to know that they can influence their own physiology, it changes their perspective and their overall belief system. I continued to teach these exercises to people for decades and worked in tandem with their physicians to monitor their blood pressure and medications to get them titrated appropriately. Most of them have become medication free.

The beauty of research, especially when it is psychology research, is that we often find solutions to problems that are fairly simple. Imagine what you can do if you believe you can influence your life and also your physical health.

Suzanne Kobasa is another one of my favorite research psychologists. She coined the term "hardiness" (in 1979) to refer to a personality trait that identifies people who manage stress very well under difficult circumstances. The importance of her research has many implications, the most essential being that there is indeed a difference between people who become sick from stress and those who do not.

The applications for us here in this program are far reaching. Imagine if you can learn how to become more proactive about your life and especially about your health and the ways in which you interpret stress. You can be resilient in this life experience and know greater joy than perhaps you have yet embraced. One formula for success is to be able to perceive stressful situations as relatively non-threatening in order to be optimistic and to better cope with situations as a result. This doesn't mean that there are not dangers in the world and in our own life, but it does mean that we have an outlook that goes beyond our fear of them, and we can believe that almost every situation presents an opportunity to learn and thrive.

Sharing this information is important here. Giving you time to be reflective about it is also important. The relaxation exercises you have been exposed to in this book are all designed to help you learn and even master how to take control of your mind—doing so makes anything and everything survivable.

"You wouldn't have a desire for a thing
if you couldn't achieve it."

—EARL NIGHTINGALE

Section III
THE CORE

Blueprint for a Successfully Intentional & Integrated Life™

Blueprint for a Successfully Intentional & Integrated Life

E ach time you work through another segment of the book, stop and give yourself time to remember that every bit of this information is contributing to your overall plan. You are placing your information onto the Blueprint and filling in the details. You need to consider what your life plan looks like in this moment, each and every day.

Are there components of life, of this life experience you are having, that you are either beginning to think about or are thinking about more deeply?

If you were building a house, we'd now be at the stage where the foundation has been poured, the rooms are laid out and timbered, the doors and windows are clearly placed, and all the electric and plumbing details are in place. We need to make sure that we like the way it looks and feels as we stand in the middle of the structure.

And is this contributing to your sense of motivation to build this best life yet through a Blueprint?

Do you think you are at this point now?

"You can tell if someone is clever by their answers, you can tell if they are wise by their questions."

Reexamining the Assessments

The best use of a test is the re-test. Now is the time to retake the assessments you did earlier. Retake them on the same page where you initially did, but this time use a different color pencil so you can track any shifts and then use this open space to write your thoughts with respect to any shifts, ideas, frustrations, motivations, and inspirations.

Assessments to review and retake:
> Mind Body Integration
> Multidimensional Health Locus of Control

UNDERSTANDING DYER
1940–PRESENT

Dr. Wayne Dyer is a bit different from the previous theorists introduced. He is a doctoral-level counselor and his training is different from what a psychologist receives. He is globally respected as an expert in understanding people and how they function.

He spent the early part of his career as a professor, but has since launched a well-recognized business writing and speaking around the globe about his very educated beliefs about how humans function and what they can hope to achieve in this lifetime.

His perspective and teachings are described as self-development. He is referred to as highly motivational and inspiring. Emerging from his adolescent experience of living in an orphanage, he found his inner strength, and he is passionate about guiding others to do the same. His messages are delivered in a calm and quieting manner and always with the obvious intent of helping people find inner peace.

His best work among the many books he has published, in my opinion, is *The Power of Intention*, a powerful book that ties together the human psyche and the laws of nature with spiritual philosophy to provide a rich and substantive program for becoming aware and powerful in this lifetime. This is an amazing work.

The central message from Dyer in this book about the intention to accomplish what you want is that it is simple—just get the ego out of the way so that you can realign yourself. The process of realignment means adjusting your belief system so that you are not defined by your material things, the list of your accomplishments, what people think of you, or by any self-imposed feelings and thoughts of isolation from a guilt about how unconnected you are to your life. Honestly, I found this difficult to grasp when I first heard it.

First, the idea of needing to place ego to the side seemed odd and even a bit offensive. However, when I stopped for a moment and thought about it clearly, I realized my reaction was defensive. Any time we have such a response, we are invited to pause and ask why. I extend that invitation to myself routinely and find it highly productive.

Dyer provides a very helpful technique about how to get into the mindset where it is possible to put ego aside and enter the zone of reception to the idea of having a clear intention. He calls it Holding on to the Trolley Strap. He relates a story of being a small boy and riding trolley cars with his mother and brothers. Trolley cars, much like some of today's rapid transit trains, have both seats and standing room. When you are left standing, you can grab onto either a pole or a strap to maintain your balance. Given that he was only a small child, the option of grabbing the strap was impossible. It was four feet up over his head.

However, as the trolley bounced around, he would use his childhood imagination to pretend he was holding the strap and that he was tall and holding on safely as the trolley would then take him safely to whatever destination he had in mind. He goes into great visionary detail along the ride to create a glorious story—as he distracted himself from whatever sort of uncomfortable feelings he had as a three foot tall kid being jostled about amongst five and six foot tall adults. He describes himself as being very internal and also hardy.

Dyer says the trolley story has application for him in his adult life and he invites us to participate.

As an adult, he creates that same mental picture of the trolley car and the reach for the strap whenever he wants to invite the mindset of intention. He envisions that strap still hanging high enough that he cannot grasp it, but he has to reach—reach very far and envision it—and the trolley is now what he calls the flowing power of intention, and he is reaching to grasp what he needs through the strap connected to that power. The imagery is clear, as is the power of the connection and the feelings of safety and comfort that it elicits. The vision of the grasp being successful enough to quell anxiety, fear, anger, and frustration and place him into the zone of relief and calm.

This is powerful.

Yes, this is a mind game. All of life is a mind game and it is, indeed, how we play the game that really matters. I find his imagery works for me, and when I utilize it, there is no way to hold onto fear or any of the negatives. Life, in its greatest moments, is always a reach . . . a reach for something meaningful in the way of a connection. Whether that connection is to a person or an event, it is always a reach for a connection.

The additional component of his messaging that I find particularly helpful is that of the completeness of the universe, as we know it, and beyond it into whatever there is. The idea of any separation between us and whatever created us, whether called the universe, spirit, Mother Nature, science, or God—is simply absent. His writings and his words spoken are about connection and extension. In the same way that we are connected to our mother and father, we are connected to our creator and one another and every living thing. Even if this seems tough to believe, just pause for a moment and invite yourself to entertain the possibility—what do you have at risk by doing this?

Keep clear in your mind that you are here because you want your best life . . . the best is yet to come, to happen, to unfold. You are reaching for it. You are reaching for the trolley strap to take you where you intend.

The additional help he extends comes in the manner of four essential steps. These are both psychological and intellectual. Of course!

1. Discipline

If we are going to be connected to others and invite what we want, we need to be connected to our own self, and that requires that we are clean, clear, and healthy. He recommends we do that by getting into a disciplined routine of taking care of our body to a productive point with regular healthy exercise and clean nontoxic eating.

2. Wisdom

It doesn't just appear with age; it is a matter of practice to gain the ability to focus and allow our self to collect our thoughts and feelings and think about how our body is experiencing that connection. This takes discipline, and together practice and discipline produce wisdom. Wisdom is paced and patient.

3. Love

The combination of practice and discipline leading to wisdom allows us the opportunity to be tuned in and to recognize what it is that we love and also frees us to believe in the experience of doing what we love and loving what we do. None of this is possible without the clarity gained from wisdom.

4. Surrender

Control is a notion we should simply abandon; influence is always possible, but the only control possible is that which we exercise in our mind, our own mind. When we operate away from insisting upon control we open the opportunity to reception.

What have you got to lose by trying to adopt this?

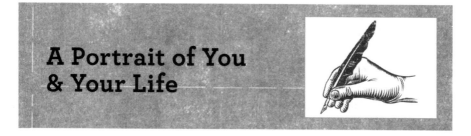

A Portrait of You
& Your Life

Your self-portrait is a revelation of your self-image and your self-confidence. As you work through the program, you may see shifts happening. Allow them. Just take each one of these exercises as a genuine invitation to look at your *self* and express it in this manner.

Go ahead, gently hold the pencil and sketch what you think is a representation of you. This is not about being the artist. It is about the expression of self for you to see yourself as you are.

THE LANGUAGE OF THE HEART

I love the idea—full blown—of thinking about the language of the heart. I am curious to know what runs through your mind when you hear that phrase, but since you cannot tell me right here and now, I'll share with you my experience.

I didn't know exactly what would come pouring out of me in this work—in my book and program. I knew that I had an agenda and it was to share with people the information, on all levels available to me, about how to find, empower, and truly enjoy the strength that lies within each one of us. I outlined the chapters and thought for several months. I then began writing and have been taken aback at what has emerged, because even though the writing is a conscious process, it is straight from the core of me.

I take a look at what I convey here and take an extra breath. I am particularly moved by how much I see my parents emerging in what I share, but this makes perfect sense. These two people who gave me my life and who raised me had conceived me in genuine love. I grew up being told this and also feeling it deeply. I know how splendid it is. I wish this for every living soul on the planet, because it is then that you begin this life journey already knowing something about the language of the heart. The problem, however, is that this is not the same experience for everyone. And so love becomes a difficult process because of the lessons already learned about how sustaining it is, how deep it runs, and how genuine love needs to be simple and pure and needs to be a lovely exchange between us.

In addition to the parts of my life that I know are happy blessings, I also know about the other things that have taken place in my life that were difficult. I have somehow, over the years, come to recognize these as blessings as well. But they are blessings I would have never invited into my world had I been given a choice.

When I was in my early 20s, my dad had a stroke. It was awful. It was the first time in my life that I had to come face-to-face with the notion that my dad was actually mortal. This sounds kind of odd to reveal, but we each do some form of this with someone we love in this world when the person is at death's door, and it takes our breath away. Here's the story and how it ties into the language of the heart.

My folks had gone to Mexico for a few weeks to celebrate Valentine's Day. They loved being away together and enjoying time remembering why they found being together such a positive experience. They had a great time; they were in their early 60s and the photos of the trip were inspiring. My dad went pair-sailing, and they had beach time and went boating and had great dining. It looked and sounded like terrific fun. However, just a couple of days after they came home, my dad woke up one morning and fell to the floor. My mom was in a panic. She surmised that he'd had a stroke of some form, maybe a TIA, but it was something to be managed immediately. This event really through her for a loop; the two of them counted on one another in innumerable ways, and when he went down, she was lost, shaken, frightened, and just plain overwhelmed. Three days later she had a stroke, right there at the hospital.

There they were, in adjacent rooms—it was very strange, completely terrifying, and also just weird. I thought that this was somehow unique, and although it is unusual, it is not unheard of. Psychologist and author James Lynch wrote the *The Language of the Heart: The Body's Response to Human Dialogue* and *The Broken Heart: The Medical Consequences of Loneliness,* and they are fascinating. What he demonstrates very clearly through physiological research is the close ties we have to one another and the basic physical impact we have on one another in good times and bad. You can walk into a patient's room when they are on a heart monitor and make some very genuine observations if you pay close attention to what happens to their heart rate and rhythm when various people enter the room and when they talk, and when they are alone, and it tells a story. To be human is to communicate—to talk, listen, and respond to other human beings. The question of interest here is about the impact that dialogue has upon our heart and blood vessels.

As a psychologist, James Lynch has demonstrated reliably and validly how simple human dialogue, the process of talking and listening to others—dramatically affects the body's entire cardiovascular system, with important consequences for health and well-being. The language of the heart is more than just a poetic metaphor for thoughts and feelings we cannot name; it is a medically established reality. What his research also demonstrates is that the heart cries out to be heard and attended to . . . and when that doesn't take place, there are tangible consequences.

We have all had an awareness of this at some level when we experience the frustration of not feeling heard by people we talk to and not feeling listened to. It does real damage to our feelings, but it goes beyond that. Remember, our mind and body go everywhere together, and you cannot do something to one without the other experiencing it as well.

The research that this man did and the way he integrated his findings into what he knew intuitively is exquisite. He reveals things that we all should know and yet somehow do not seem to know. It is that we are so vital in our being and so in need, genuine need, of real love between us and understanding and appreciating deeply that love. We need to tend to it and treasure it, for our happiness for sure, but also for our health.

I remember that when I was happily married, a friend asked me how I knew that the man I had married was really the right one for me. My reply was that he felt so good next to my heart, and he never gave me a stomachache, not in any form, not when we were together and not when we were apart. And I loved his voice. I loved climbing into his arms and just being there. His voice, his tone, his pitch, his words, all soothed me regardless of what I was doing or when. The language of his heart to mine was spot-on, it was beautiful. This is what my mom and dad had; that was how I first knew about it and how I knew we can all have it.

Love of all kinds and the love in our relationships takes much knowledge. We each are faced with having to learn to deeply love our own *self*. You're finding that to be true here in this series, aren't you? It is a good awareness to have and to embrace because when we do that, when we begin there, we have something powerful to begin to take hold and blossom.

You've been reading about the self talk you need to do. This is another dimension of the reality that is essential to tune into, because when it comes to the core of life, it is about you and how well you deal with *you*. It is about how much you can love *you* and be with your own *self*, your own body, your own mind. The people we love the most are those who really love their own self really well. This quality is very attractive. What is not attractive is when people play the role of something less healthy, such as the victim or the bully. That is not about loving yourself healthfully, and those types of people are very difficult to love and relax with because the language of their heart to ours and to their own *self* is very twisted and unsettling.

In Dr Lynch's work, he raises the question about why it is that people have hypertension. It is a disease that is in epidemic portions here in the United States. We attribute it to many factors. In my work, I teach people Dr Herbert Benson's Relaxation Response because I know full well the benefit of helping people to take time and relax their entire body and mind. Interestingly, however, Lynch finds that it is not just the exercise that is productive. It is the voice of the person and what that voice conjures for the listener that makes the most significant impact. The voice of a loved one will be very meaningful if there is goodness in that relationship, at the very core. There is also a way to provide comfort with your voice by the tone, volume, pitch, and passion you impart with it. I've found myself becoming increasingly more aware of my voice and my impact as I work with people as I gauge their response to me given how I use my voice.

Lynch and I are in deep agreement that when people have a disease, we need to remember that the word itself—disease—can be broken into two words–dis ease. This means a level of discomfort. It is vital to tend to this discomfort at every level. He asks himself, with every patient, what it is that they cannot express and what it is that their heart longs to ask for, to say, and to obtain. There is a link, really many links, between where we are when we are happy and in love in terms of the state of our heart and where we are as far as our happiness when we get sick and are in a state of dis-ease of the heart.

When a baby screams, what do you hear?

Although it can be frustrating, listen to hear what the baby needs. Babies are not manipulative. They are babies, and that means they are in a state of innocence, and they cry out of need. Guess what, so do we.

We need to tune into the baby and also one another when there is any form of cry expressing a need, any need whatsoever.

When I was a teenager, I volunteered as a recreational therapist at Children's Memorial Hospital in Chicago, my hometown. It was months before I discovered that I was working in a terminal patients' wing of the hospital. I innocently went there every day and listened and observed and played with the kids. They were sweet, and they were so ill. It was so difficult, because no matter how sick they were, they always wanted to play. In reflection about those experiences, I look and see the ways in which adults and children can be so far apart from hearing one another.

There is no reason for it; we need one another. We get joy and security and love form one another, but first we must listen and then talk in ways that mean we are communicating with a knowledge and appreciation of the language of the heart.

What do we do to ensure that? Everything up to this point in our program to find the strength within has been to prepare you to listen enough to yourself to be able to hear your own needs. That's where it begins: to be gentle and loving enough with your own *self* to make time to fulfill your needs. And from there, to reach out to others, all the others in your world, close and near, intimate and not so much. Listen, really listen, and watch faces and nonverbal gestures. Keep your heart open; get out of the way of seeing what is there to view. Listen, watch, and receive. Deliver your love, let it come from within you, from deep within you. It is the strength within you that is love.

Your Self Talk Script

Sit here now, and listen to your own language of the heart. Feel yourself embraced by words as they come from your outer self to the core of you, the real you, the you that is so eager for deep love and respect and appreciation—the real you that would love to trust enough to know you can receive every bit of love that you crave, that you desire, that you'd die for. Envision it. See it. Know how gentle it is in one moment and yet at the core, it is strong like nothing else. Love runs deep. Love is the strength within you. Allow it. Breathe. Stay here, knowing you can allow every portion of love to come from you that there is, and there is a powerful amount. Allow it, know your strength.

To view the video: www.drdebcarlin.com

Journaling Exercise

Can you feel the impact of your willfulness?

What does it look like?

Describe your own intentionality here, and write what your desire, that is, what your intention for your life is.

What is the language of your heart?

How do you speak it and when?

INTIMACY WITH SELF AND OTHERS

What is intimacy? What comes to your mind, right to the forefront?

For me, it means being completely naked—and being loving—loving in every physical, emotional, and psychological sense.

I love that imagery and also love the experience, but that scene is actually sometimes easier to achieve than any deep and meaningful conversation that occurs on the backside of that experience. Have you found that to be true? Yea, of course you have, because just like everything else here, that too is part of the human condition. It's strange and awful and it takes a whole new kind of awareness to get from one kind of intimacy to another and from what we have with our own self to what we have with another. Vulnerability is at the core of the fear.

In the 1960s and 70s, a group of women wrote a book entitled *Our Bodies, Our Selves*. It was revolutionary. And wow, what an eye opener back then. This book, which was about an inch thick, told women everything they didn't know and often didn't even want to know about their anatomy and physiology—*every*thing. They went so far as to have women get hand mirrors and position themselves for self-exploration. I thought it was both odd and also fascinating. When you think about it, why should anyone know your body better than you do? How can you possibly live in your own body and not know every part of it? Well, you can, but why wouldn't you want to know what is yours? If you feel uncomfortable with it, how will you ever be comfortable with anyone else knowing it whether it is a healthcare provider or a lover? The simple truth is that you won't feel comfortable—ever. That sort of discomfort, dis-ease, leads to a divorce from a portion of your *self* and that means a distance between you and the intimacy of you. This is a basic setup for a health compromise. It is a position of jeopardy for you, for any one of us who puts anything between us and our *self*. This is a fun little play on words here, but I am serious and this is not gross or unhealthy or weird—it is just about you. And you can keep it very private and just think about how you know your own self.

Do you run from your thoughts or do you engage them? Do you *self* talk? Do you know your body and why it feels the things that it does, or do you ignore your symptoms, your experiences, and run to someone else to tell you what is going on, but only when you get really frightened? Can you imagine what life could be like if you knew you better than anyone else did? And if you knew your own *self* that well, how much better could you know another and be connected to them?

Intimacy with the *self* is the place to begin to further your awareness of being close to you and then others. There is also that passionate intimacy between lovers, but that is not the only type of intimacy that there is to know. I also think of intimacy in ways that are less intense and vulnerable than that initial image, because intimacy can take place in every relationship that has any degree of depth to it. You just don't take your clothes off and become sexual about it, but there is that level of vulnerability, that special degree, that element of closeness that occurs when we go deep to deep—as I have mentioned in earlier.

There are some wonderful people writing great stuff about essential conversation, meaningful dialogue, going deep to deep—and it all hits me as on-target for what we each need to do. The process and the details of what it all means can be explained in a whole number of ways but, at the center of it, there is a revealing. There is genuineness. The game-face is off. The agenda is about sincerity, it is pure. It is about being emotionally available as well as being psychologically available to another, and the desired outcome is *knowing*—knowing the other person and knowing your own *self* that much better because of the connection and what is illuminated as a result. It is a way of being nude with your clothing on your body, but being respectfully naked to truth . . . and what is honest.

This is important because almost all of us have comprehension. We know what is there, what is present, what just *is*. We know it because all reality takes space. Whether it is physical space or psychological space or emotional space or intuitive space, it is there taking space. When we have conversations where the truth is not spoken, it is frustrating. If we have weak self esteem, we feel doubt about our perceptions even though we know somewhere inside of our own *self* that we should not have that doubt. If we are of strong self-worth, we just get agitated and find fault with the other person for not being honest, or we create a story to take them off the hook of accountability. In either case, it is not satisfying. We crave being honest with one another and not having that be injurious.

I remember when I was in high school, there was a turnaround dance. The girls were to ask the boys on a date for the dance. In that era, it was a big deal to ask a guy out on a date. I had a boy who was sort of my boyfriend. I wanted to ask him and he knew it. I knew, sort of, that he would say yes, but the asking was like me jumping off the Hoover Dam with a bungee cord on. I was not interested in the risk or even attempting it. I remember being with him at a sports event at the school and he kept leading the conversation to make it easy for me to ask him, and I kept on dodging it. I felt like an idiot for playing the game, but I felt awkward. He finally looked at me and became very direct: Debbie, do you want to ask me to the dance? You know I will say yes.

Thank goodness he was more capable of intimacy and courage at that moment than I was, or it wouldn't have happened.

That evening taught me a lesson. I didn't want to feel myself in that position again of wanting something but feeling myself standing in the way of it happening. Standing in your own way—what a concept!

We do it all the time, don't we? We do it with our lovers when we crave something physically. We do it with our partners when we want them to behave in a different manner but cannot find a way to let them know easily. We do it with our bosses, employees, co-workers, with all those performance reviews that take place every day across the nation. Is anyone out there doing them really well? Does anybody actually enjoy them? They are painful!

Why?

The why of it is that we hide so much stuff from our own self that we feel like we need to bury our self in front of anyone else, it's burdensome. Even when people do that 360 evaluation, there is fear and trepidation because we get fearful about what we might end up being told.

In my career as a psychologist, wherever it is that I am working, whether in a home, a hospital, a school, or an office, my clients pay me to be honest and to look at the situation they are in with my professional training and say what I see taking place, including how I see them in the midst of it. That night from high school stays with me. Funny as that may seem but I need to summon my courage all the time; I seek my inner strength daily. I need to know *me* well enough to be able to count on my self to assess what I observe and then to share the seeing with who wants to know what that view is. It always sounds weird to me when I describe this, but people consistently seem to understand what I am talking about. This is because it is a scene we all know, and, it too, is part of the human condition.

I need to tap my inner strength to do the work I do, because I believe it is the right thing, but I used to become afraid sometimes when I am trying to be helpful. I don't want to injure anyone in any manner. I am also billing my clients; I don't want them angry at me because of the news I deliver. It has taken a lot of inner work to be intimately comfortable with my own self to be able to arrive at the place where I can guide others to trust me to take them on the journey of seeing, of hearing, of listening, of then speaking so we can go deep to deep with one another to become vulnerable, to take the risk and allow what will be to happen, to unfold. Whatever it is, it will be honest and we will deal with it.

My life is better since I began to live it this way. I've sought people to help me learn this, to guide me, to teach me, and it has been vital. This can be for you as well.

And when my dad died, it was really vital to know this. As I stood there with my mom, holding her up to face what was happening, she knew her self well enough to know what was coming. She knew how to release my dad from their earthly intimate connection back to his intimate connection with his self, so he could transition into whatever that space is that we go into when we die.

It scared me. I hated it, but I did it again when my mom was dying, and it is important to be able to do for those we love and then for our own self when it becomes our time. I cannot make the plea here any stronger than to say to you that it is my heart's desire, my passion, to help you feel you can be so delightfully intimate with your *self,* and that you will find great joy in it and will then be so much more able and capable with another. This is your life, this is—it.

Your Self Talk Script

Stay here. Envision *you* in every splendid way, with your every dream being realized and embraced. Know that you know every portion of you and that this is beauty filled. No other person can take that knowing away from you or cause you to question it, because you know you, you love you, and they will love you if they are worthy of you. But you will be discerning, and you will make good judgments because you want peace and happiness and fulfillment; this will be yours.

This is all leading you into having depth in your life as never before.

To view the video: www.drdebcarlin.com

SELF-ASSESSMENT
Speed of Trust

Stephen Covey tells us that it is the speed of trust that changes everything. Trust issues affect everyone, everywhere—at home, at work, all around the globe. Trust means confidence and you know it when you feel it. When you have trust in someone, you have confidence in their abilities, their values, their judgments, their abilities, and their loyalty. Every bit of trust impacts the core of a relationship. Without trust, nothing gets done. When trust is high, things happen fast and effectively.

Let's take a read on trust right now. Well use Covey's tools from his book, *The Speed of Trust*.

Think of a person you have a high level of trust in; it is a high trust relationship.

Who is that person?

Describe the relationship.
    What's it like?

    How does it feel?

    How well do you communicate?

How quickly can you get things done with one another?

How much do you enjoy this relationship?

Who is responsible for this relationship? And how is it maintained?

Now think of a person you have a low level of trust in: it is a low/no trust relationship.

Who is that person?

Describe the relationship.
   What's it like?

   How does it feel?

   How well do you communicate?

How quickly can you get things done with one another?

How much do you enjoy this relationship?

Who is responsible for this relationship? And how is it maintained?

The difference between high and low trust relationships is enormous. You can't have success without trust. The word trust embodies almost everything you can strive for that will help you to succeed. You can't reveal to me any human relationship that works without trust, whether it is a marriage or a friendship or a social interaction; in the long run, the same thing is true about business.

The Economics of Trust: It Is a Simple Formula

Trust always affects two outcomes—speed and cost. When trust goes down, speed will also go down and costs will go up.

$$\downarrow \text{Trust} = \downarrow \text{Speed} \uparrow \text{Cost}$$

$$\uparrow \text{Trust} = \uparrow \text{Speed} \downarrow \text{Cost}$$

Think here for a moment. What happens when a marriage breaks up?

How about a business relationship that ends badly?

Things fall apart when trust is lost and everything takes longer to accomplish as a result.

PLAN OF ACTION TOOL

Trust

1. Obtain *The Speed of Trust* by Stephen Covey (2006)

2. Establish 4 Cores of Credibility:

   Integrity-walk your talk, be congruent

   Intent-have your motives clear, honorable, straightforward win/win

   Capabilities-hone your abilities, be 100% credible

   Results-get the right things done

3. Adopt the 5 Waves of Trust:

   Self Trust-have self confidence, set high goals, keep them

   Relationship Trust-establish trust accounts with consistent behavior

   Organizational Trust-focus on credible alignment, be directionally on

   Market Trust-allow your reputation to be trusted and be trusting

   Societal Trust-give back, be charitable, inspire

4. Dedicate yourself to taking action in a more deeply committed manner to create change, to inspire trust

Behave   See

Speak

The way in which we see things, speak about them, and behave either inspires or destroys trust.

CONTINUING THE DANCE OF LIFE—WORK BALANCE

In my line of work, people come to me because they are in some form of trouble. The trouble is either about their personal or their work life. Very often it is about the trouble they are having taking care of these two very different parts of their life, both of which are important to them. For most of us, our work life is not just about money. It is about self-esteem and self image. The work we do makes us feel proud and respectable. However, our core sense of worth in this life comes from our personal foundation, our most intimate relationships, the families that we create, and the people we love. Without close relationships where we give and receive love, we are lost because life has no depth or genuine meaning. Our hearts need to be as fulfilled as our minds.

In our current culture, perhaps more than ever before, there is a pressure on both men and women to create a home and also create a career. Creating a home includes the reality of having a family, but the complication sets in with the questions of who will take care of the children? Who will tend to the domestic sphere to make it the place of respite and comfort and true nourishment that we all need in order to rest and prepare for the next busy day? And who will create the earnings to make the domestic environment everything we want for it to be?

Both sides of the equation of our lives are filled with variables and tensions. We are placed into positions that become uncomfortable when we have to make choices about where to expend time and energy and resources. Very often the tension that is created is shared with our partner and loved ones in ways that make us feel as though we are neglecting obligations. Worse yet, is when our loved ones make it clear that they are feeling left out because of the obligations that don't concern them. Over time, feelings get hurt, perceptions form that harden the heart, and our relationships suffer as well as our individual health.

I've yet to work with anyone who has told me that his or her home and work life is perfect. Each of us seems to be pushing to make everything fit and to ensure that all parties are happy. Well-being, however, cannot be manufactured by creating an illusion—it either exists or it does not. The answer to this enormous challenge in our lifestyle is simple: it calls for honest reflection. You know when you look into the mirror and look into your own thoughts what the condition of your life is. You even know your own prognosis for happiness and illness. The tendency, too often, is to run and hide from the truth we know. My pitch here is that there is no place to hide—and that is the blessing.

Everything we encounter is actually some form of a blessing, an opportunity to learn something new and tune into our life well-being. There is nothing more important.

Your Self Talk Script

Sit quietly. Breathe in. Allow your self to envision what you do now for a living, for your work, and how it produces income. Stay here with it and attend to what the feelings are inside of you no matter what they are. Just hang in here with this, and allow it. As you are here, right now, is this what you want? Or do you have a desire for something else? Is there another picture of you coming into view? Can you see your self in some glorious light of happiness and fulfillment? Can you feel your self in a position where your life makes rich sense and you feel a satisfaction you have been craving? Pay close attention to this and extend compassion and patience to your self. You can make anything happen. Reach down into your core and feel the strength within you; it is there, it is your self-love, it is your dedication to who it is that you want to be. Allow it. You can find it and obtain it. Keep what it is in your mind's eye, and know that where your thoughts go, your energy flows.

Breathe, relax, envision, commit . . . it'll unfold, if you allow it.

To view the video: www.drdebcarlin.com

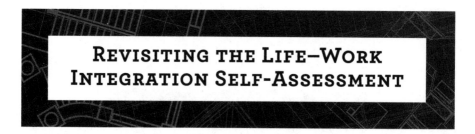

REVISITING THE LIFE–WORK INTEGRATION SELF-ASSESSMENT

This should look familiar to you. You've worked through this same notion earlier. You're invited to revisit it again here because this is a tough, recurring theme.

Business is very personal. We take it to heart when we get hired, fired, evaluated, or when we are included or excluded from a meeting, a team, an event, or a decision. There is nothing about business that is not personal. Period.

This works both ways. Each of us is a whole person. We take our head and our heart along with us wherever we travel to. If there is trouble at home, it spills over into the workplace, and everybody knows it. Try to cover it up and people talk about your weird behavior. If you become ill, you are sick both at home and at work. Where we go, our stuff follows.

The opening question for you here is: how well integrated are you between your personal and work life?

Think about your answer as you reply to the questions that follow.

Answer honestly. If you don't, then this is just a silly game that is a waste of time, especially yours.

1 = not at all   9 = all the way

1. I am an integrationist between my work and personal life.

1   2   3   4   5   6   7   8   9

2. I am a separatist between my work and personal life.

1   2   3   4   5   6   7   8   9

3. I am completely functional; there is no awkwardness at all in the way I deal with personal and work life.

1   2   3   4   5   6   7   8   9

4. I am confident the people in my work life would agree with my assessment.

1   2   3   4   5   6   7   8   9

5. I am confident that the people in my personal life would agree with my assessment.

1   2   3   4   5   6   7   8   9

PLAN OF ACTION TOOL
Where Are You?

Look at the pictures below. Pretend the picture symbolizes you. Visualize what parts of you are where; for instance:

> what parts are at your work life,
>
> and what parts of you are at your personal life,
>
> and what parts of you are integrated into both?

Use color to help you see this clearly. Use the colored pencils and just point to or circle the various parts. One color is for work life and one color is for personal life. If colors overlap, this is okay. This is simply your own representation of your inner perceptions.

Take a moment and think about what you just created in the way of a visual for yourself.

Is it the best you?   Yes   No

In order to really know what the best *you* is and can be, you need to be overtly aware of your values and your rules. List here what your values and rules are.

PLAN OF ACTION TOOL
What's Important?

Your values and rules are closely tied to your passions. Getting a clear and tangible picture of your passions is essential because our passions drive us. Fill out answers to the categories below.

What I love
(What I must absolutely have in my life)

What I hate
(What I won't stand for in my life)

What excites and drives me
(What I am most passionate about)

What I am committed to
(The results I must achieve)

As you look at what you have listed, and also look at how you colored the picture of yourself and the ways you have identified the parts of you that are invested in your personal life and your life, think of how you need improvement in both and list them. Just start with five in each.

PERSONAL AREAS OF IMPROVEMENT

1.

2.

3.

4.

5.

PROFESSIONAL AREAS OF IMPROVEMENT

1.

2.

3.

4.

5.

Now look at which one you have more to write about, your personal or your work life . . .

Or are they 50–50?

ENVISIONING YOUR FISCAL WORLD MINUS FEAR

It's been my experience that although people talk about being short of cash, there is just as much fear, and sometimes even more fear, around having cash and meeting with financial success. Money is a funny reality; it is not just paper and coin. It is about ego. It is about value, self-worth self-perception, and our placement in society. It concerns impressions about what having a certain amount of money means with respect to where you live, where you spend your time, who you spend time with, and how accepted you are into a circle of people or how rejected you are. There is a lot of emotion wrapped up around money.

I grew up completely clueless about money. All I knew was that there was stuff, good stuff, all around me—a solid house, all the creature comforts, new and reliable cars, attractive clothing, good schools, great social activities, and fun vacations. I didn't have a grasp about how it all happened.

When I was a youthful, smart-alecky adolescent, I left home prematurely, rented an apartment—a sublet, actually—and began a course of my life which was quite illuminating and really hideous. When the landlord, about two months into the renting, realized that two young girls had sublet the place from his tenant and of course we had not paid the rent, we thought, what do you mean we need to pay the rent? He came over for a visit and we were really insulted at his behavior and decision to evict us.

I was equally appalled with the utility companies when our services were discontinued because we had not paid bills. I promptly made telephone calls to them announcing who I was and informing them that my parents had been long-time customers, good customers, and didn't they realize who I was? It's embarrassing to recall my ignorance and also my arrogance, but it is a true experience and I had to learn from it. By the way, took me decades to learn how to be reasonable and handle money and pay bills and think about investing cash and being smart. It has taken even longer to realize my better understanding about money and how to obtain it, retain it, and sustain it—plus grow it.

America is producing people now who are in even worse condition psychologically about money. We have an entitlement attitude amongst our citizens that makes me look less foolish about my youthful journey. What's this all about?

Although I have a variety of political opinions about this topic, the core focus here is about how you can envision your fiscal world, your finances, and your money minus your fears. Money is merely a thing that shifts hands, sometimes a lot and sometimes infrequently. The problem for too many people is that it shifts hands too frequently; they get money and rapidly need to disperse it, and the complaint is often that there is an imbalance in the incoming and outgoing. I understand this.

However, what I have come to know from working with some people who are poverty stricken and others who enjoy great wealth, is that there are fundamental mindset differences, extending way beyond knowing how to work to make money and having a whole lot to do with our attitudes. The very phrase "poverty stricken" is telling.

A man I knew very well who had grown up in poverty espoused his hatred of poverty, and as a result he hung onto every meager amount of money he created. Each payment he received from clients was swiftly placed into a bank account. He would add up his deposits daily and would keep a running record across the day of what he was earning and what his expenses were. He was so tightly focused on the details that he was looking at things in a microscope and missing the bigger picture. He saw only one way to produce revenues for himself, and he was so dependent upon his client base for payments to keep his bills paid, he refused to do anything that might upset them and cause them to look for another provider of his service. As a result of this, he wouldn't raise his rates for at least a decade, and then only made meager increases. He lived on the edge all the time, nervous about the money, living like a pauper.

No doubt you are familiar with the current terminology about abundance. There have been a flurry of books written about the subject of how we think and behave about having an abundance of what we need, and just as many programs created around these ideas. Some of them are great and others are a bit frivolous; they are frivolous because they miss the point about really understanding the essence of abundance theory.

Abundance theory, in simple terms, is essentially about trusting that you will find what you need because the world has plenty of everything available, always. Throughout history, however, we witness things of value being scarce. When things of value become scare, human beings adopt a preservation mode of thinking where we want to hang onto whatever it is we think we need to have just in case it is hard to come by the next time.

This kind of thinking leads us to ration and hoard. The reality about scarcity is not about a lack of something in existence, but is about finding a way to obtain what is there. Although there was a Great Depression in America in the last Century, not everyone experienced the depletion. People who lived in the urban areas and who worked for companies that were failing had a very different experience from family farmers who produced their own foods and supplies and weren't dependent upon a paycheck to eat. Abundance is about scarcity, demand, and availability, and it's also about creativity. There are simple models of it and also very complex ones—economists have had fun with this topic.

As described in Wikipedia, the following model, which is a favorite of mine makes the theory of abundance sensible. Sensible over trendy is what I aim for.

> "The **Heckscher–Ohlin model (H–O model)** is a general equilibrium mathematical model of international trade, developed by Eli Heckscher and Bertil Ohlin at the Stockholm School of Economics. It builds on David Ricardo's theory of comparative advantage by predicting patterns of commerce and production based on the factor endowments of a trading region. The model essentially says that countries will export products that use their abundant and cheap factor(s) of production and import products that use the countries' scarce factor(s)."

At this level of functioning, it is about a political and economic game. People who are the consumers simply get caught in the game.

At this stage in our culture, gasoline prices fluctuate greatly. Is there a scarcity of fuel? Although you can argue on either side, the tangible fact is that there is an abundance of fuel, but there is a tight fist holding the spicket to ensure that demand remains high and that prices remain high as well. Gas prices for automobiles generally increases during the summer when it is well known that Americans like to get into their autos and travel. This has fuel producers happy as they anticipate being able to gouge the drivers because they will be demanding a substance they need for their pleasure experience. Most of the time, this tactic works.

However, times are shifting a bit and people are deciding to experience "staycations" as a result of not wanting to live in a scarcity mode, but would prefer to experience abundance by entering into a new mindset: let's not run to another part of the country to see what is there. Let's enjoy what we have here, since there is so much. Some people even wonder why they see things now that were unnoted previously.

When, for whatever reason, we have to turn our attentions to appreciation of what is actually here, we see more of it.

I look out into the world and see a need for everything I offer. I see an endless supply of people eager to live a better life and to hear from a person like me what my stories are and what my tactics are for creating an existence that produces happiness, wellbeing, and satisfaction. I see shifting from one format to another as freeing me to explore, not limiting me. I envision money as a fair trade for what I offer and that line of thinking all hangs together to produce what I need and crave.

There is an element of this that feels esoteric. That's okay, because so much of life is that way. We simply need to sit in the middle of it and allow it to sink into our thoughts and into our perceptions.

The other most important aspect of money is self-worth. Do you feel like you would be out of place in your current world if you had a lot of money? I've often heard people chide those who have money by asserting commentary about how snooty people are—how arrogant, and how uppity. This is our perceptions gone awry, because that attitudinal observation can be made in any class level in our culture. I've heard people talk about how money corrupts people. It's not the money, it is the attitude with which you handle it. This is all of why it is vital for each one of us to do our self talk and be congruent with our core self. We need to work to remain grounded and clear about our values and integrity.

In order to have our fiscal affairs in order, we need to be clear about what financial comfort means to us and what we want from money we obtain—what does it buy us? Are we looking to purchase more things or to rest easy knowing bills are paid, or are we eager for extravagance? The knowing will lead you into where you'll become productive.

Your Self Talk Script

As you are sitting here, attend to what thoughts and feelings have emerged from within you. Examine where you felt easy and where you felt tension.

Do you know how much money you have today? Are your bills paid? Do you have a stash for times when you want to kick back and not have to work to keep things alive? Are you running to keep up on payments for the things you have? Do you envision yourself sitting comfortably and enjoying all of the luxuries in this life, all the things you value, all the things you would love to have. Can you do that exercise? And when you do, where is the money factor?

Think deeply here, and breathe, relax, envision, get clear on your thoughts and your feelings, and remember to extend kindness and compassion to your self as you encourage your self to focus on what you desire to obtain. Where your thoughts go, your energy will flow. Be positive; believe in abundance. Know you can have whatever you desire. Have faith. The ladder is your reach. Be in the stars, pull back a piece of the sky. It is yours to do with as you wish.

To view the video: www.drdebcarlin.com

SELF-ASSESSMENT
Your Fiscal Comfort Zone

Money is more than just coin and paper. It means something in terms of our self-respect. It influences our self-image and overshadows our lifestyle.

Do you know why? Do you know what role money plays not just in your life, but in your head?

The opening question for you here is: Is money what you want or is it something else?

Think carefully, reply to the questions.

Answer honestly. If you don't, then this is just a silly game that is a waste of time . . . especially yours.

1 = not at all   9 = all the way

1. I have a great, high-trust relationship with money.

1   2   3   4   5   6   7   8   9

2. I am able to live my life without worrying about money.

1   2   3   4   5   6   7   8   9

3. I am completely in need of more money all the time.

1   2   3   4   5   6   7   8   9

4. I cannot envision my life where money is genuinely abundant.

1   2   3   4   5   6   7   8   9

5. Having a lot of money means you are greedy and that's ugly.

1   2   3   4   5   6   7   8   9

6. If I had more money, I would then be able to be generous.

1   2   3   4   5   6   7   8   9

7. I have a vision of myself all alone if I don't have money.

1   2   3   4   5   6   7   8   9

PLAN OF ACTION TOOL
It's More Than Currency

Do you earn your own money or does someone give/gift it to you?

Have you ever made and also lost a lot of money?

How much money do you want to have in your bank account in one year?

What do you want your net worth to be in one year?

What net worth do you need to be in order to feel comfortable?

What net worth do you need to have to feel wealthy?

What is the most amount of money you have ever had at your disposal?

How did it feel?

PLAN OF ACTION TOOL
"Think & Grow Rich"

Obtain a copy of *Think and Grow Rich* by Napoleon Hill, originally published in 1937 and one of the best-selling books of all times.

Read all 15 chapters and adopt the ideas. The author is a powerful influence globally on the subject of money.

1. Thoughts are things
2. Desire
3. Faith
4. Autosuggestion
5. Specialized knowledge
6. Imagination
7. Organized planning
8. Decision
9. Persistence
10. Power of the master mind
11. The mystery of sex transmutation
12. The subconscious mind
13. The brain
14. The sixth sense
15. The six ghosts of fear

Take the Self-Analysis Questionnaire for Personal Inventory.
There are 28 questions.

Get out paper and pencil and calculator answer the questions and
also calculate your monthly expenses and work the math as directed.
Remember, it is just math, and you can control it by your actions. If you
don't have your own money, create a plan to get it . . . with passion and
integrity.

Remember your values. Write here what you want your money relationship to be.

Write here what you now see as a potential threat to your financial
well-being.

Write here what a potential solution might be.

Write here what you are willing to do to commit to the plan, the solution
for your financial freedom.

"Whatever a man can conceive and believe,
he can achieve."

—NAPOLEON HILL

Section IV
TAKING IT TO THE NEXT LEVEL

Blueprint for a Successfully Intentional & Integrated Life

Reexamining the Assessments

Understanding Palmer

A Portrait of You

The Faith Factor

Self-Assessment: The Faith Factor

    PLAN OF ACTION TOOL: *The Faith Factor*

    PLAN OF ACTION TOOL: *The Relaxation Response*

Nature, Time, & Your Connection to the Earth

Journaling Exercise

Life As A Cycle Intended, Not Happenstance

Self-Assessment: Expectations of Success

Plan of Action Tool: Expectations of Success

Self-Assessment: Movement & Desire

    PLAN OF ACTION TOOL: *Expectations of Success*

Stress Managed Is a Life Well Lived

Holmes and Rahe Scale of Stress

    PLAN OF ACTION TOOL: *Creating a Plan of Wellness*

The Plan of Intention for Our Life

Blueprint for a Successfully Intentional & Integrated Life

When it is time to take it up a notch, you have to be ready. The question for you here is—are you ready?

We're moving through the pages and taking various looks at the self and allowing time and opportunity to be just flat out *self*-focused, and it is all good. And how can it possibly be anything less? Your connection to your own life and the *you* that is living it is essential. The connections that you have to others on this journey are essential.

As you build the structure that is your Blueprint, you need to bear in mind that the inspectors will be looking closely to ensure that everything is in good order, ready for you to inhabit that place and be safe. No matter who you might want to pay off for a clean sweep, there are penalties you cannot escape if you cut corners. We've got the talent, the materials, and the budget is not stingy. We can afford to reach and get the best of everything you want here.

Excellence is a term to embrace. It is what we can feel we are in search of as we stand on the tips of our toes to make something happen. It is that extra stretch, that additional push, and that preparation that we know instinctively will make the entire deal a whole lot better.

Take it up over the top here in this segment. Select the colors and the hues you really want to live inside of. Make those window treatments everything you have envisioned and coveted when you've seen them elsewhere. Go ahead and install the rain forest shower, the Jacuzzi, the indoor sauna, the outdoor hot tub, the heated pool, the outdoor kitchen. Just do it and do it with the faith that it is all what it should be.

This is your Blueprint. You are the architect and you run the tradesmen and the design teams. Everybody is eager to hear your intentions. Share your vision and be clear about it. Reach down deep and come out with your very best—this is your life. Map it.

Reexamining the Assessments

The best use of a test is the re-test. Now is the time to retake the assessments you did earlier. Retake them on the same page where you initially did, but this time using a different color pencil so you can track any shifts. Then use this open space to write your thoughts with respect to any shifts, ideas, frustrations, motivations, and inspirations.

Assessments to review and retake:
    Speed of Trust
    Continuing Work–Life Integration
    Your Fiscal Comfort Zone

UNDERSTANDING PALMER
1939–Present

Parker J. Palmer, born in Chicago, Illinois, he is a well-respected author, educator, and activist who focuses on issues in education, community, leadership, government, spirituality, and social change. He earned his doctoral degree in sociology at the University of California at Berkeley.

One of Parkers best-known works is a book entitled *The Courage to Teach* (1997). In it, he makes vividly clear that it is our educators who shape our lives just as essentially as our parents. It is our educators across every portion of our life span that imprint upon us our sense of worth and self belief about our ability to learn and to embrace the idea of lifelong learning.

Parker is well versed in the areas of man's humanity. He is an important voice for us to hear because of all the ways he understands society, sociology, humankind, our relation to one another, and our process of learning. His work transcends generations and his wisdom has impact in the most dynamic ways. He is well known and respected for the work he has done to deliver a powerful message about the importance of having courage. His facility, the Center for Courage & Renewal, is a place where people from all walks of life can come to learn how to tap their inner courage and become more deeply connected to others as a result.

Palmer talks about the need for each of us to have a life that is balanced between bring quietly secluded for reflection and one that is vibrantly engaged with others. I was first introduced to his work from my client that was a school district where the educators and administrators read *The Courage to Teach*. They were attracted to his ideas about how the educator impacts the student beyond formal classroom academics. He talks about the reality that the interpersonal connection between the educator and the student has a powerful impact on what learning takes place.

This resonates with me. Even as a small child I knew that if I liked and felt a mutual respect in my relationship with my teacher, I would have a strong desire to learn and to demonstrate my achievement. If I didn't have a healthy rapport with my teacher, I recoiled because there was a fear factor present and I did my best to avoid the instructor. I've witnessed this repeatedly in the schools and districts I have worked with. I've also learned that this concept can be generalized and applied to many other situations—the truth is that having an accord and harmony with others matters.

Parker is very approachable. I was so inspired by his writings that I initiated communication with him through letters and then e-mails and phone contact. We quickly formed a rapport that has been a friendship lasting over a decade. He is now in his 70s and his work continues with energy and insight and a determination to help people find the best of who they are inside their mind and soul to ultimately benefit how we connect to one another and do outstanding work for our society—both local and global.

As described below in my book *Between Magic & Logic: An Educator's Compass For Clarity & Renewal* (by Deb Carlin & Wynn Miller, 2004) Parker offers us a pathway to understanding one another by using his techniques that are consistently designed to take us more deeply into our thinking and feelings so that we can realize our best self to be more genuine in our teaching. Regardless of our profession, his words are applicable to any career choice and our personal life at every level.

> In his book, *The Courage to Teach,* Parker Palmer writes about how critical it is for each and every educator to recall the passion that initially brought them into the profession of teaching. Regardless of how cynical we may sometimes feel about life or events, we each live in our heart . . . we want to connect to people and we want to connect to what it is in this life that gives us a sense of purpose. When we feel passion for our vocation, for the job we are doing because it gives meaning to some aspect of life and to our culture, we experience a confidence that exudes from us . . . it is knowable by us and it is viewable by others. Leaders, good leaders who are effective and have people who look up to them, have passion and they have a vision that they share. As an educator, you can share the vision you have for your people (child and adult alike) as you get to know who they are and what their dreams are.
>
> In the midst of educating, it is important for us to have clarity about this kind of reality because when we don't, our ego can interfere with being able to help another person—fear about

being left behind when a student excels beyond us, fear about not being able to make a meaningful difference for our student, fear of revealing ourselves to someone we are in charge of—you can add to the list with what your anticipation of fears for yourself or others might entail.

The point is that unless we are clear inside of our own self, our competencies are easily shaken; we need to have them firmly grounded by having our feet upon the ground. Grounding comes with self-awareness. Your inner landscape is a beautiful place and it needs tending to. With tending, it will flourish and you will reap the benefits.

What does thoughtful tending look like? Parker Palmer was explicit regarding a problematic dynamic of the human condition, which is unfortunately evident in many academic cultures: seemingly, each teacher was "put on earth to advise, fix, and save each other, and whenever an opportunity to do so presents itself, we should seize it!"

How many times has someone come to you with a concern, and your first instinct was to give advice? How many times have you sought to share a concern with others only to be given a quick fix? Our question for you here is how does this kind of dialogue contribute to the important grounding we need to do in order to achieve self-awareness? The answer is that it doesn't. Superficial fixing does not generate a climate of mutual consideration and relational trust, which are two prerequisites for the grounding of self-awareness through collegial support.

Parker Palmer makes a critical and important point by stating what the belief has been for so long in terms of fixing, yet he also shares another approach as a balance. It is one that offers the educator a chance to educate their colleague by helping them think and feel critically about their issue and use selective, community inquiry to seek resolve. He describes a technique used by the Quaker community clearness meetings.

CLEARNESS MEETINGS

Clearness meetings are a way of bringing a group of people together for the benefit of one person in particular. The object of the meeting is to help the person who requests the meeting, obtain a new level of clarity through non-threatening questioning: a process framed by specific guidelines for all the people involved. It is a unique and interesting way of sharing an experience of coming together for some one in particular.

The purpose of the clearness meeting is to offer another tool for gazing through the window into the soul—in a non-threatening way, and in a way that allows the foundational process to move ahead with new kind of confidence. Palmer offers the rationale for such an experience:

> "If we want to support each other's inner lives, we must remember a simple truth: the human soul does not want to be fixed, it wants simply to be seen and heard. If we want to see and hear a person's soul, there is another truth we must remember: the soul is like a wild animal—tough, resilient, and yet shy. When we go crashing through the woods shouting for it to come out so we can help it, the soul will stay in hiding. But if we are willing to sit quietly and wait for a while, the soul may show itself."

A model developed by the Quakers many years ago provides the framework for such work. Beginning in the 1660s, it has proven to be a time-honored process that is invitational and respectful, and helps participants—as a community— lay the groundwork for solving problems.

This is not a "fix it session"; we employ the same touchstones described earlier.

A clearness meeting offers the potential for solutions by insight that can be gained by the use of inquiry. Each person simply asks questions, non-threatening questions, in an effort to help the person of focus think critically and strategically about his or her stated concern.

Each of us is well aware of the vulnerability that such a meeting can arouse. However, few of us are fortunate enough to have had the setting within which to be a part of such a format. When handled compassionately and with positive and thoughtful intent, it is a very satisfying way to gain insight and build relational trust.

When we conduct the program, we do these kinds of meetings within the context of the program. No one is ever pressed to be the person of focus; as the program designers, we are the initial volunteers and we teach you by modeling this wonderful, Quaker technique.

The work done in the clearness committee has a simple set of guidelines or rules all of which are governed by an overarching principle: *everything done in the context of a clearness meeting is done in strictest confidence.* In fact, double confidence must be followed. This means that at the close of the meeting no one in the group should approach others regarding any aspect of the meeting, be it about content or the group dynamic. *No one* can waiver from these guidelines before or after the actual meeting . . . not if this approach is to work and be effective.

The rules are simple in design, but require close adherence to their intent. There are 9 rules in all. It is helpful to ask everyone to recall these 9 rules as they gather, sit and prepare to begin the process—reading through these rules is not advised; it can be regarded as offensive and a bit demeaning to people who already understand them and this whole approach is about trust . . . and trusting one another's abilities and sensitivities.

1. *Group membership:*
The person seeking clearness ("focus person") chooses about three–five trusted people. Diversity of the group should be one guideline that is thought through carefully: age, background, gender and so forth. Most of all, the invited need to be people with whom you believe you have relational trust.

2. *Focus person preparation:*
The focus person is asked to think about his or her issue of con-cern and be ready to orally present them in a about a five minute or so format in a helpful way to the small group.

3. *Group member obligations:*
The meeting should last for about 60 to 90 minutes. Clerking is done by everyone in the group; this entails reminding everyone of the rules, closing the meeting on time, monitoring along the way, and making sure the rules are followed. Also, someone (or all) in the group take brief notes, which are given as a gift to the focus person at the close of the meeting.

4. *Meeting format:*

There is an initial centering silence and the focus person, when ready, may break the silence with a brief summary of the issue at hand. At this time, the committee members may speak, but under one unchanging rule: the members are forbidden to speak to the focus person in any way except to ask thoughtful questions that are not baited but are sincere. This means the questioner can not try to disguise advice or their own personal agenda in any way. This technique simply doesn't allow room for that; it is a different kind of thoughtfulness and the rules are stringent in order to help facilitate critical thinking and relational trust. The consistent goal of any clearness meeting is to help advance the focus person towards his or her own inner truth.

Centering Silence is simply having someone in the group, anyone, bring the meeting to order by asking for a collective silence and calming . . . close your eyes, sit for about 3–4 minutes and then the same person asks if everyone is ready to begin.

So what does an open type of sincere question look and sound like? As Palmer describes, "The best single mark of an honest and open question is that the questioner could not possibly anticipate the answer . . ."

Questions should be framed to help the person of focus, not the questioner's personal curiosity.

Questions should be brief and to the point and involve feelings as well as facts.

Questioners should trust their gut instinct—even if it seems obtuse to the task at hand.

Examples of an open question:

As you sit silently and think of the issue, is there a part of your body that speaks to you, and if so, what do you think that means?

When you envision a solution, is it somehow controlled or free flowing?

•❖ *Try to come up with a few examples of an open question on your own:*

As you sit here thinking about the situation that prompted your desire for this particular forum for some kind of resolution, what ran through your mind with respect to what input you would obtain here?

When you think about the root cause of this particular situation, can you envision a pathway that heals everyone involved?

5. *Role of the focus person:*
The responses to the questions should be full but not lengthy. Keep in mind that the more questions and subsequent answers the more material the group will have to work with. The focus person should assume total power regarding limits of the process—the focus person may choose not to answer a question.

6. *Role of the group members:*
The process is not a grilling exercise. The pace should be relaxed, gentle, and humane. Silence is more than all right, it is good and should be trusted within the process and may mean that a deep processing is unfolding.

7. *Group member disposition:*
Everyone must focus on being totally attentive to the focus person and his or her needs: no chitchat, responding to others, joking, or nervous laughter. All are present with their respective attention and care. If the focus is broken, the person who broke the rule needs to be immediately reminded.

8. *Closure process:*
The meeting should not end early because there are no more questions—patience evokes deeper questions. With about 20 minutes

left, the focus person is asked if he or she would like to suspend the "questions only" format and begin a mirroring process. (Mirroring allows the group to reflect on the focus person's language—and body language—to see if a response surfaces.) Mirroring, if allowed, does not necessarily end questions. With 5 minutes left, members of the group should celebrate and affirm the focus person and his or her strengths.

Mirroring is a simple technique but it requires some practice so the mirroring statements don't sound offensive to the one being mirrored. The most essential way to learn and develop this skill is to practice with friends in an open and overt manner and get feedback. The idea with mirroring in a Clearness Meeting means that the use of inquiry is still employed.

Examples of mirroring:

I noted that when you talked about your work, you were animated and seemed to come alive. Did you note that?

Each time the topic of retirement surfaced, your voice pitch intensified and became more emphatic. Did you note that?

➥ *Try to come up with a few examples of mirroring on your own:*

Celebrating the focus person's strengths, means finding kind and genuine comments to make about them at the end of the session, not clapping and leaving abruptly. After a session of being vulnerable, it is important to ensure the focus person leaves feeling authentically positive.

Examples of celebratory comments:

Your willingness to engage in this process demonstrates your strong commitment to being courageous and tapping into your inner strength—this is fabulous!

Your caring responses are a tribute to your beautiful sense of who you are in your core and also to the professionalism that you exhibit.

➤ *Try to come up with a few examples of celebratory comments of your own.*

9. ***Meeting outcomes:***

Remember, the meeting is not intended to fix anyone; therefore, there should be no sense of "letdown" at the end: a good clearness process does not end—*it* continues to "speak" to the focus person in the future. An underpinning of the process is that all members believe the focus person will gain wisdom through his or her inner teacher.

The clearness meetings, if you'll allow them, have the power to help you get clarity in ways that are astounding. You have the competence to engage. You have the competence to be the productive receiver at the meeting. You have the competence to be a productive contributor to the questions for someone else at their meeting.

➤ *If you were to call a clearness meeting today, what would the topic be?*

➼ *Do you know who you would want to invite? And why? It is important to reflect about the people you select and be very clear about what you believe about them. This may sound simplistic but doing so can give you additional resources to understand how to cultivate others into your life and into this experience:*

What follows are some thoughtful ways for you to tap into yourself . . . take the time for yourself and answer privately. You may discover you desire a meeting focused on your request for clarity about something.

SPECIFICS

➼ *What is it that you do and know you are good at?*

➼ *Was that answer in the personal or the professional realm first? Can you answer for both?*

➼ *What is it that you do and know you are not good at?*

➼ *Was that answer in the personal or the professional realm first? Can you answer for both?*

➥ *What is the difference between the person you are and the person you would like to be?*

➥ *List, in order, the most significant events of your life that have contributed to the person you are today . . . beginning with "when I was born . . ."*

➥ *Is that you? If no, why wouldn't it be?*

These last few questions tap into your level of confidence and this work is, in part, designed to help you realize, really recognize, what you are good at and what you can be good at. All of that comes from knowing of your own self. Once you know yourself, you can be genuine and authentic with your audience, whether they are your students, your children, your colleagues, or your loved ones. And as a result, your relationships will have a relational trust that is full bodied and very rich.

The techniques described here are important to fold into any life plan, any Blueprint, because they are about the core of us. We benefit when we commit to develop the skills that facilitate not only our inner clarity but the manner in which we can become clear with others.

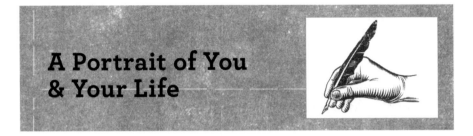

A Portrait of You & Your Life

There are certain exercises in life we can never afford to grow tired of. They include routines that are physical, cognitive, psychological, spiritual, social, and emotional. And if we crave being whole and being healthy, there is no such thing as skimping on *self* focus. Selfish gets a bad rap—if you don't focus upon your *self*, who will?

Take another look at who you are and how you are perceiving your *self*. Allow this exercise to be a barometer of how you are feeling, and where it is that you fit into your life, your picture of you and your life.

THE FAITH FACTOR

I never wonder, not seriously anyway, why it is that things happen—no matter what those things are. This is because when I am patient and contemplative, it always turns out that there is a reason of some sort to be discovered and an opportunity to learn something—something that is useful and important, even when I'd rather not. That's kind of a tough concept for us human beings, no matter how highly evolved we become in our consciousness and in our heart, because there are events that take place which we object to. They seem wrong and senseless and unfair. We have a great desire for fairness. The phrase "that's not fair" must be one of the most frequently used string of words on the planet, and we often use it nearly as much as the statement "I don't want to judge anyone, but . . ."

When I was child, I was introduced to religion in a variety of ways. My mother, who was of Polish decent, was raised as a Roman Catholic. My dad, who was of Swedish decent, was raised as a secular humanist. This was an interesting combination. Across the life of the time I had with these two magnificent people, I must have had literally thousands of conversations with them about faith, about what they thought, what they believed, what they felt, and what they observed. You'll note that I did not include in that statement "what they knew." The knowing part of faith is almost an oxymoron, for faith and knowing collide; they don't really run together. That's why there is no argument to be had about the topic. It is about belief, not tangible evidence, not really.

So why bother inserting it here in this series?

The answers to that are numerous, and I hope you find them illuminating for your heart, your mind, and your soul because the strength within is all about learning how to outfit that inner part of you to be the very best, most satisfying and productive—*you*.

Although I went through the traditional route of Catholic upbringing and received the traditional and well-timed sacraments of the church as a child, I was also invited by my parents, especially my dad, to explore the religions of the world and make my own informed determinations about who I am and why. I was also invited to explore what I believe and embrace and why. He didn't want for me to inherit my faith; he wanted it to be mine. He wanted me to embrace it and have it be useful to me.

I began by reading, and in those days there was no Internet or Amazon.com to order from. You got books from the library. I was also sent to various vacation Bible study sessions during the summer when I was in grammar school. Let me assure you, I thought that was a contradiction in terms. I thought vacation was about beach time, not Bible stuff.

However, my childhood friend, Juanita Deterding, and I got hooked into all sorts of things that our mothers, who were one another's closest friend, thought was a good idea. So I went to a Lutheran Bible Study. I've thought often about what those times revealed to me. Mostly, they taught me songs and introduced me to the concept of being alienated from others by religious identity. When kids found out I was Catholic instead of Lutheran, there was a bit of distance between us and some teasing about the Blessed Virgin Mary that Catholics are known to hold in high esteem and pray to. Thankfully though, these were good kids, and we moved on quickly to find ways to simply be children and play together as kids. The lesson however stayed within me.

I recall other scenarios, such as being in a public grade school where each Wednesday afternoon the Catholic kids would be called to the front of the room to line up and then march over to the local parish school for our catechism lessons. That seemed odd too. I always wondered what the other kids in my classroom thought about who we were and where we were going to each week. There was never any discussion about it, but as an adult, I am curious as to whether the teacher offered up some form of explanation. And in the 1960s we, of course, stood together in our public school classroom and said the Pledge of Allegiance to the flag of the United States of America together, and no one ever opted out, even though we all said together that we believed in God. Life was simple then. I was, essentially, raised in a rather homogeneous community and people didn't make an enormous fuss about religious differences.

I don't know that we had any awareness about how it could divide us until the 5th grade. That year we had Sheri in our class. She had transferred to our school, and she was immediately liked by everyone.

We all became friends in the class. Things rolled along just fine until Halloween and we found out she couldn't come to school that day and participate in the holiday: in fact, not in any holiday, not even birthday parties. The message I was given from my parents was that it was a part of her family's religious conviction not to. This was stunning to me. It made me feel sad. And I wondered what the God I was raised to believe would object to. It got me thinking . . .

At summer camps, through the YMCA, I met and became friends with kids who were Jewish and who lived in the very Jewish shopping district of Chicago. We had all sorts of fun, and we talked only a little bit about our religious differences in terms of Christmas and Hanukkah. We envied one another's practices but it was not about religion. It was about ceremony and the elements of fun and gifting. Again, my mind became busy with what all that meant.

In high school I went to a small private school, lovely place. There were good people in charge, and I made great friends there in addition to sharing the experience with my childhood friend, Juanita Deterding. You have to know how much I love that name. Can you imagine what fun it was to sing such a fun name out loud when I was about seven years old? In that educational experience, our faculty invited us to study the religions of the world and, in our senior year to write a thesis about what our religious convictions were and why. The reason for the assignment was to have us, during those adolescent years of identity development and awareness, understand why we took on the beliefs we adopted.

It was an amazing journey and very revealing. And it was the first time I had ever given heartfelt attention to the reality that we adopt, for the most part, the religion that we are born into, or we just reject it and forgo adopting another. Lots of people take in strong convictions without really examining the merit of them. In fact, it is considered offensive to even suggest that it might be wise to. If you are finding yourself offended here, please be patient and understand that this is about enrichment, not a challenge of beliefs.

As the world becomes an ever-smaller place, we are bumping up against one another's religious beliefs, and, even more, we are colliding with perceptions and misperceptions.

For college I went to state universities, again pursuing philosophy and also understanding and knowledge of religions, and then also studied psychology because it all seemed to tie together for me. Alongside history and anthropology, and sociology and political science, everything about religion and beliefs is connected to the region people are from and their family history and community. These tie us to those we are in close proximity to, and it prompts our behavior and our beliefs. But the question became for me: does it prompt, influence, motivate, or even inspire our faith?

Faith is a whole other topic, or at least another dimension to the topic, and it is often left over to the side—to the side while we learn the literature and the belief structure for any religion. We study the practices and the routines and the ceremonies, but it is the meaning, the richness, the center of beliefs that I am focused on here. And in my life experience, what it has meant is what I can share with others from the language of the heart.

I've attended different types of houses of worship, from temples and churches to outdoor settings that are meditative, in many different parts of the United States and other countries around the world where I watch, observe, listen, and ask questions. I ask people what their faith is . . . not what their religion is, but what their faith is—what is it to them, what do they believe, and how have they come to believe it? I have extended this to Himalayan yogis way up in the mountains whose faith literally puts them into a position physically to defy what we know as reality, such as placing their body into a small 1 cubic foot box and closing the lid without panic or injury. Or they place a sail needle through their arm and play it like a violin but produce no blood, no pain. This is not about their religion, but is about their faith factor. It's weird and amazing stuff.

I've found this to be a very uncomfortable topic for people, overall, unless I release them from having to back up what they believe or feel. I invite the conversation to simply be about belief in terms of faith. What do you have faith in?

Do you *know* what it is that you have faith in? What do you believe?

When I went through my graduate school experience, I studied at both Saint Louis University, which is a Jesuit organization and at Washington University, which is a secular institution. The environments were each rich, and I made note of the differences they embraced and the practices I observed in both places. However, I found faith and also a lack of it in both places and sometimes from the same people. I found convictions, ones that ran deep. Why is that? What is there to become defensive about with respect to the topic of faith and what is there to be so nonchalant about with respect to this topic? I find people at the extremes but rarely in the middle.

In my readings, I have found a number of authors to be particularly helpful. Wayne Dyer is perhaps the most helpful of all, alongside Paul Pearsall. There is also Herbert Benson and Joan Borysenko and Thomas Moore, and these are really just a few. There is a lot of great literature to review and gain meaning about the nature of faith. These people write and speak about the value of faith, not in terms of religion, but in terms of having a belief in something very magnificent and powerful outside of our own self. They refer to the power as God or the Source or Nature or the Universal Influence. It's not about the politics of religion. Sometimes it is hard to get into a conversation about faith because of these other factors of organized religion and politics. But for here and right now, I invite you to simply let go of that. Keep whatever convictions you own, but walk here in this pathway for just a bit.

Across this series, I have talked about life, childhood, parental relationships, sickness, death and coming into a psychological state that is natural and life affirming. Life becomes affirmed for us through emotional intimacy—through love. Life is significantly less meaningful if it is without purposeful activities or genuine depth, and if it is without magic.

Purposeful activities are the ways in which we actually spend this time we know as our daily life. Genuine depth is the connection we make with others that touches our heart and spirit as well as igniting our mind. The magic to me is about splendor, and also about miracles. What are these things known as miracles? I think they are everything from the reality that we are here, to the healing of an ill or injured person in some mysterious manner, to the moon rising, and to any and every invention ever created by man. Faith is the factor that makes it all happen. Some of it is faith in the self, and some of it is faith in some unknown and mysterious force we cannot explain, not really.

Research for many decades indicates clearly that having faith beyond one's self and this immediate life reality has a positive impact upon the human experience in tangible ways.

It influences our health when we relax about having to control everything and manage every outcome, for we have faith that there is another force at work. It influences our blood pressures and heart rate and rhythm as well, and *that* is at the center of our being and our wellness. When we believe faithfully, there is no argument or necessity for defense. It is just a state of comfort, of embrace.

When people ask me to defend my faith, my response is consistently relaxed as I willingly admit that there is nothing to defend. My faith is based in my heart and it makes my mind feel good. It is just a way of existing and being and it brings me joy; it brings my blood pressure into the realm of healthy. It keeps my heart beating regularly, and it is pure; it is not speculative. It just *is*.

When I am asked to defend what leaders in any faith do, say, or enact, my response is that they are simply human beings, simply mortals. They are trying to live in a role within a religious system and they too are searching for faith, for a place to be comfortable, and like all of us, they meet with failure too often. No excuses, no explaining—we are humans. We do good things and bad, every one of us, and some more than others, but when you stop to think about how we all arrived here, there is no conflict to be argued about over evolution versus creation. They can exist simultaneously. Why not? What is the harm? Nothing. What is the implication, really, of an argument there? It achieves nothing productive.

I am a psychologist, yes a social scientist, but I was first a physical-science scientist—studying pre-med and I loved the biology and chemistry, and every component of it. I never, even then, saw the need to defend varying ideas of how we all arrived here. It all fits; don't resist the idea and the picture will have a chance to emerge.

I cannot envision why it is critical to argue about faith when it is so clear that we need a release from feeling as if we need to be in charge of everything in this life—how it happens and when—and from needing to answer the "why" of any portion of it. When you stop to consider that we have far too many heartaches and feelings of loss and despair across all of humanity, it seems reasonable that we could and would all benefit from the thought and faith that there is indeed some reason, some positive reason and healthful explanation for everything that life brings, both the sorrows and the joys.

What if, just what if, we are here from the Source, whatever that Source may be, and it is a good thing, a thing of love and depth and beauty—a beauty as deep and vast as the globe and the entire universe. We came from it and evolved from it, and our life experience is to enrich it in return for our experience here. What if, in that line of thinking, we are here to be pushed up against and to encounter whatever it is, and to make best use of our resources, the inner resources that we each have to find opportunity to understand at a new level. And then to embrace, to behold, and to grow from using everything that is there for our senses and our sensibilities to interpret about why we are on a certain pathway with the specific encounters that we experience.

How about if we look at the issue of faith as an investment in all of humanity and the globe, a tie that binds us to one another for an experience we are all in—this life. What about sharing the coming from some beautiful source and landing in some virtuous place when this experience transitions into the next. What is there to lose with this way of thinking? Especially when science makes clear that there is a benefit to our health, we have nothing to lose.

Your Self Talk Script

I invite you to sit here and to be contemplative, meditative, prayerful . . . to envision the entirety of *you* in a place of peace and relaxation, of calm and of knowing, of being so clear and loving inside of yourself from all of your journey here with self talk and clarity that you can feel the strength within you as a vibrant and meaningful source. Let it become you. It attracts all of goodness to you and allows you to infiltrate each magnificent portion of life. You do good work every day. You have faith. The faith factor lives in you and around you. You don't have to control; you aim to have an influence, but there is a knowing that you are participating in something wonder-filled and lovely. Whatever it is, it is life-giving and also life-sustaining.

Sit here, breathing naturally and knowing. Focus on one—one life, one inner strength, one being—to invest in as a factor of faith and core knowing. It frees you to become. Breathe in life and love and health and knowledge. Just feel.

To view the video: www.drdebcarlin.com

SELF-ASSESSMENT
The Faith Factor

We are here on this planet and the question looms large over humanity—why are we here? Many ask and also argue about how we all arrived. There is good reason for us to tap into what we think about this topic.

This is your life; this is all about you . . . what do you know about your *self*?

Answer honestly. If you don't, then this is just a silly game that is a waste of time—especially yours.

1 = not at all   9 = all the way

1. I am determined to accomplish what I identify as important to me.

   1   2   3   4   5   6   7   8   9

2. I am clear about what it is that is important to me.

   1   2   3   4   5   6   7   8   9

3. I am a person of faith—faith in a power greater than my own self as a human.

   1   2   3   4   5   6   7   8   9

4. I am a person without any conviction on the issue of faith.

   1   2   3   4   5   6   7   8   9

5. I have great confidence that faith is nothing but fodder for the weak.

   1   2   3   4   5   6   7   8   9

PLAN OF ACTION TOOL
The Faith Factor

When thinking of faith, do you put it in terms of God?   Yes   No

Were you raised in any particular religion?   Yes   No

Did your religion add any value to your life?   Yes   No

Why or why not?

What are the goals you set for yourself last year?

Did you accomplish them?   Yes   No

Why and how . . . OR . . . why not?

What are the goals you set for yourself this year?

Are you on the path towards accomplishing them?   Yes   No

Do you have a path?   Yes   No

What is the path?

What are you willing to do to make it happen?

PLAN OF ACTION TOOL
The Relaxation Response

There is research that indicates very clearly that **The Faith Factor** has an enormous benefit to the mind and the body. Both medical and psychological research on personality characteristics and belief systems demonstrate that those with a strong belief in a power greater than themselves cope more effectively than those without this trait. The benefit extends from their degree of positive reduction of stress to benefits to their immune system and their enhanced cardiovascular capability.

Dr. Herbert Benson, a cardiologist from Harvard who established the Mind Body Institute more than twenty years ago at Bethesda, has researched this phenomenon for decades. I've studied alongside him; he was very generous with his time and talent and encouragement when I worked on my master's degree thesis research.

I taught patients who were diagnosed with hypertension how to do Benson's Relaxation exercise and shift their physiology through their mindset training to the point where they would lower their blood pressures. Collaborating with the patient's internal medicine physician, we were able to titrate them off of their medication and sustain normal pressures as long as they retained the practice.

In his pioneering work on hypertension, Benson was determined to create an exercise that mimicked what the yogis do to achieve a state of mind and body rest that would be palatable to the American population. He created a simple exercise and wrote with Miriam Z. Klipper the book to accompany it titled *The Relaxation Response.*

In this simple exercise, we have demonstrated reliably and validly that blood pressures can be managed successfully (minus any organic damage) when the mind and body learn to work together to relax. Amazing. I strongly recommend that you make the purchase of this book and learn his methods even though there are many others available.

At www.drdebcarlin.com we have a page of video and audio for you to listen to so you can achieve this state of relaxation in ways that I have refined over the years of practicing and teaching Dr Benson's original exercise.

A Meditative Exercise for the Mind and the Body

To achieve a state of relaxation, it is essential that the mind and the body work together to relax them in unison. Do this exercise at least 2 hours before or after eating so that your body is not competing with where the energy ought to be spent, that is, digesting versus relaxing.

1

Find a quiet place, a place where you will not be disturbed for at least 20 minutes to begin the exercise, and allow 30 minutes for the meditative exercise once you develop the habit, which will take about a week. Select soft music that has a 20-minute time frame. It will help relax you and also track the time for you, so that you are not time watching.

2

Place yourself into a comfortable seated position on a chair, and lean back, feet flat upon the floor, with your arms resting next to your thighs or on the arms of the chair.

3

Close your eyes.

4

Envision in your mind your entire body sitting and looking very peaceful, quiet, and comfortable. Breathe naturally and easily with your mouth open slightly so you can take breaths easily. Be natural.

5

Retaining that vision of being relaxed and comfortable, begin a journey through each part of your body. Begin with your feet, then your ankles, calves, knees, thighs, hips, buttocks, gut, chest, back, shoulders, upper arms, elbows, forearms, wrists, hands, neck, head, face, kidneys, liver, stomach, heart, and lungs—telling each to relax and feel comfortable and rested and warm, and with blood flowing freely through each in order to be healthy and vibrant. Do this dialogue for each component listed. Take your time; this exercise is your gift to your self.

6

As you continue this journey through your body, you will find
your mind trying to take you elsewhere. Keeping it on a leash is
simple if on each exhale you quietly say the word ONE
to yourself, even in a whisper. Repeat the following: This is
one exercise for my one body, in my one life, one . . .
one . . . one . . . my mind and body are one.

7

As you arrive at your head, focus on each part of your face and
instruct your jaw to unclench, your brow to relax, your mind to
be clear. Sit quietly, repeat the word one and the script above.
Allow your body to remain in this state as you continue to
breathe naturally. You will know that it is time to slowly come
out of this state when your music ends but you will do it slowly.

8

Gently move your hands, wrists, arms, feet, ankles, and legs.
Open your eyes and reorient as you move your head gently from
side to side and feel the loosening effect of the exercise.
Stay seated for a few minutes. You need time to readjust
and prepare to resume a pace of activity.

NATURE, TIME, AND YOUR CONNECTION TO THE EARTH

There have been so many humans who have taken the time to study, write about, and talk about what they find in nature and time and their connection to the earth. It is ironic that we become so disconnected from nature and the time of nature and our connection to the earth that we come to the point of needing to isolate our self from it.

We are alive here as a product of nature and the cycle of life, but we complain about the way that nature behaves, and we want more ways to predict it and even to control it. This is amusing at so many levels. Again, the idea of control is in the forefront and control is an issue about convenience. It is about having what we want when it suits us. I want sunshine and 75 degrees for the 4th of July, and I want snow for Christmas. Okay, I've placed my order but may receive neither. In actuality, it keeps things interesting.

The issue of both nature and time are important for us, increasingly more so as we remove our selves and our self further form natural time and nature with every convenience. Trust me: I love convenience, but I also want an awareness of what the implications of that are.

I am fascinated by how time has come to control so much of our living experience. We set a clock to define time. We follow it and we count off minutes and seconds and hours. Although this is useful for a whole range of cultural reasons, we often lose the capacity to let go of that artificial awareness and just relax and tune into what nature tells us about time—from the rising sun, the rising moon, and the tides of the waters around the globe.

In some sects, people believe that women are more closely tied to nature and a different kind of time element because of monthly cycles and labor and the delivery of children, perhaps, that seem to be somehow influenced by the moon and also barometric pressures.

Human beings are often blind to what nature offers and more obtuse than creatures who will warn us of events of nature such as impending dangerous weather. We just have to know from their behavior how to tune into their messaging to us.

When I still lived in Chicago in Lincoln Park, my husband loved it there and enjoyed the beach of Lake Michigan daily. But we also were passionate about having a garden. We had a tiny one but since we were able to grow veggies and flowers, it made us feel healthy and happy. We worked hard at it. We turned the earth in the spring when the ground thawed from the winter. We saw the birds return to the area as we worked out in the quiet of the garden. We saw the bugs that lived out there, and somehow they were not as icky as when I saw them in the house. Here they had a purpose. We got filthy dirty and exhausted and covered in mud on the days it rained on us. We loved it. It was joyous and the weather then seemed to never be as big a deal as the years now when I am less garden-oriented and more invested in what is going on outside.

A good friend of ours met a man, a very wealthy man, and they lived in a gorgeous penthouse downtown. Since he had grown up with nothing but poverty, he vowed to never get his hands dirty again as he accumulated increasingly more wealth because he associated it with the memory of being "dirt poor." The problem was, however, that he became increasingly more depressed as the years went by and he continued to be ever more successful.

As simplistic as this sounds, I invited him to come over and have dinner and enjoy a nice evening of garden dining and moonlight fun. He accepted. Granted, the company was great and the food and wine were fabulous, but what got to be really invigorating was the adventure we took with him—and for him—of sitting right there in the garden on a stool in the dirt right beside a plant. We had a cold bucket of water, sharp knife, sauce, and napkins. The event was very casual, very dirty, really, but fresh. We carved our dinner from the live plants and cleaned them right there and dipped them into a sauce that was spectacular and laughed about getting grubby. He had his hands in the dirt within an hour, crumbling the soil between his fingers and laughing and by the end of the evening, he was wanting to arrange a party in the rain so we could make mud pies. His life shifted gears—he was not dirt poor, he was filthy rich, and it was great and we all laughed, really happily and hard.

I have in the back of my yard, which has a pretty nice-sized garden, a big fire pit. It is a place where I build roaring fires. I guess it is about 150 feet from the house through a nice stone pathway in the garden. If I arrive when it is cool or even freezing outside and I need a break, a relief from time and from civilization, I walk back there, casual and ready. I lock up the front of the house, close the gate to the property, turn off the phones, light two candles outside, build the fire, and sit. I look at my house and it seems so far away because I am sitting vulnerable out in nature, alone with the flames and the sky, and the bugs, whatever they may be, and little creatures and night birds. Sometimes it is a little scary, but it is life and I embrace it. I don't look at any clock. I allow time to slip by me, and I sit in the enjoyment of a pureness of life. I always feel fortunate when I spend time out there, when I give an evening, a long night to my self to watch the moon and gaze at the stars for hours, with no agenda, just being. It is rejuvenating.

I do a similar thing in Chicago by getting into a sailboat and going far out into the lake, Lake Michigan, and sitting there loving the fish I see and the birds and sunshine and the quiet, and the loudness of nature and the wind. I am reminded of how I can influence direction but not ever really control it. I am there to cooperate with nature and work the sails and the rudder to get where I desire to be. I never book my time out there on a clock because I know the adventure is a day, a long and exhilarating day.

Whenever we can return to the earth and connect and believe what it is that we have faith in, we place our mind and our body into a position of hearing a bit differently, and having a full circle experience abut life and being-ness. It is potentially splendid because it places us into a space where we can hear our inner voice and feel that inner strength, which seems to me is so very tied to the natural world. I think that is why we love animals and are fascinated with watching nature. That's good but we need to also feel it—live.

The most fascinating and terrifying experience I ever had was one I took on at the suggestion of a dear friend who was a midwife. She was certainly tied to nature in her line of very natural birthing of babies. She suggested that while we were on a trip up in northern Michigan that I have her drop me off in the deep woods . . . alone . . . and that I spend the night solo, and remain there for about 36 hours

One bag, with no change of clothing. One little lean to tent, a small sleeping bag, a little pan and pot, a few tea bags, some cheese and crackers, a water bottle, toothbrush—not even a mirror, but matches. Yes, matches, and a flashlight. We weren't completely nuts. However, no mobile phone.

Yikes.

This was an enormous challenge to take on, for every reason running through your mind right now. I was frightened but also excited. If

I could live through it, I could do—gees anything. But could I survive this? I mean, really?

What if I started crying or got sick or someone tried to murder me or big bugs came at me. Or a wolf or a bear? What if I just freaked myself out?

I took the task on. I got out of the car. I walked for what seemed like a long time and found a bit of a clearing. I sort of knew where I was and I thought I was pretty clear about where my friend would meet up with me sometime the next day, but the whole time-frame was a bit fuzzy with no watch or and real commitment for any exactness in time. I set up my little ground and claimed it my own very quietly. I remember being very frightened and crying a little when it got dark and I heard things in the woods and felt like I was being watched—that was the worst part and also the best part, because I thought perhaps no one really nuts would be out in the woods. Maybe what was out there was—oh just use your imagination here—for all that my fantasy life produced for me that night and morning.

The point is that I think I need to do that adventure again and routinely because there is nothing that can possibly empower you more than time alone with the earth, with nature, and no barrier—at least not substantial barrier.

My thoughts and my fears were right there with me. My life didn't flash in front of me as though I was dying, but it ran before me as though I was in a movie and was being asked to both watch and critique. It was time to think because there was no distraction, just me and the earth and all those earthly things. Owls hooted and so did other birds, and things flew around me. I swear there was a bear out there, and a wolf or something howled. I've always been prayerful but that event caused me to pray to understand my place in this world, my place on the earth, my position amongst all other living creatures. I really felt my inner strength emerge as I fought and then relaxed and examined my fears. It was refreshing and exhilarating. It's been years since I called forth that memory, but the experience was awesome and power-filled.

Have you ever done something like that?

Do you ever even spend a night all alone, and in all-quiet?

When the power used to go out in my neighborhood before power lines were updated, I'd end up with a few nights of inconvenient darkness made bright by candles and writing on a tablet of paper with a pencil and pretending I was a colonial-times girl. It is amazing what pours forth.

Your Self Talk Script

I invite you to take time and to lose time in nature. Reflect about your position on this earth among the many others. Where do you fit in? What if nature was suddenly there with no amenities? How would you think and how would you feel?

Close your eyes and imagine you are a Native American and you are living 200 years ago. You farm and hunt and live off the land in a tribe with primitive, humble homes. What does it feel like to watch time in that era? To follow the sun and the moon and the stars? Who do you become that is more powerful than the person, you, who is here now? What strength emerges from within you that is the primitive portion of your *self*?

Sit, breathe, envision.

To view the video: www.drdebcarlin.com

Journaling Exercise

Our interior is described as primitive with raw emotion. Do you find yourself feeling raw emotion? If so, what are those emotions and where do they come up from?

If primitive is wild and animal-like, what animal are you? How untamed do your emotions feel to you? And are you interested in taming them?

When thinking of primitive, animals, wildness, and taming, it is impossible not to think also about nature and our ties to it. How do you experience your ties to nature and the natural cycles of the earth?

What role does faith play in your thinking and feeling?

LIFE AS A CYCLE INTENDED, NOT HAPPENSTANCE

Although an argument can be made for the belief system that life just happens, there is just as much evidence that the power of intention has a meaningful impact upon the quality of our life experience.

We each come into the world with a certain degree of welcome by whoever it is who receives us. We are then placed into the hands of people who are charged with being the providers of our care until a time when we can begin to attend to our own needs. Unfortunately, there is no criteria for who gets to be the care provider of the innocent—when you birth someone and the infant becomes your responsibility. This seems unfortunate, because, in my mind, we do not own anyone, especially the people we bring into the world. We are simply here to serve them, to ensure their safety, their comfort, their lifelong development, and their fulfillment to society as a contributing member.

However we are raised, we develop notions about how we influence the world around us or how we are held captive by our world. Some learn early on about the reality of intentionality and others never seem to understand the connections, but it is never too late to learn.

There are misconceptions about intention and what it means, what it is, and how one behaves in intentional ways. The popular perception seems to be about a forcefulness, a push, a thrust for making things happen, but that is not what I mean here. Here, having intention is about becoming a part of something, a universal energy, a force that is invitational, not demanding. The mindset comes from the spirit within us—a spirit created through a universal source that guides us, if only we allow our self to tune in, and listen, and allow. The model is about allowing, not forcing. It is about attentiveness and listening, not demanding or pushing. Intention within this model is creative and loving and abundant, but it takes an openness, a receptiveness in order to connect into it.

If you think about how it is you believe you are set into this world experience, you will no doubt have thoughts about some sort of an energy, a feeling, a weird kind of experience of intuitiveness that is always present but mostly unexplained and certainly intangible. This is simply a human experience. We all have this to a degree, and we share it, albeit often unspoken. There are many things in this life that are intangible for us, but we know somehow that they are real, and they exist. The question however becomes: where do they exist?

The best answer I know is that what is intangible for us is what exists all around us. It is some sort of an energy, a force, a source, a being, a way of being that is just simply life. We come from it, we live with and around it, and perhaps we return to it when we die. I don't claim to know. What I do know, however, is that only some people get in touch with it during their life experience and when they do, it seems to make a phenomenal difference in a very positive and powerful way.

Human beings have written about this for . . . well, forever . . . the mystery of life, the mysterious forces of life.

Why are so many people removed from whatever it is that is the energy of life and from this concept of connectedness and intention?

When we examine our development, at least in countries like America, it seems apparent that our ego is a main ingredient in sidetracking our intuitive energy because our ego both invites us and then also allows us to think that we can be in charge and manage just about anything. And over time, that creates a distance for us about what is natural and intangible. Over time, we dismiss what we cannot see and our ego becomes ever more prominent.

Think about how it is that your ego interrupts your ability to be connected to other people. We're great at this—we get offended by others, we feel disrespected, we believe we are more important and should be heard. We stand in the way. That's what all of that is about. We stand in the way as we somewhat innocently protect the self from insult, from injury. The problem is that when we do that, we don't see the whole picture, for the whole picture includes seeing the self as very connected to others and able to understand where the ego has a healthy place and where it becomes a tool of isolation and defensiveness.

All of this is strange subject matter and its weird to wrap our thoughts around and get into on a feeling basis, as well as a thinking one, but when we allow it, we can see that who we are is not about what we own, what we achieve, or what others think of us. We are simply a part of everything. We own what we have with everyone, and our accomplishments are a collaborated effort, across many. We cannot set our self over to the side of anything, not really, because we are all joined together in this life.

Esoteric as it sounds, the beauty of this thinking is that if we keep it simple and avoid our own skepticism, we can tap into what we are already a part of and what we are primed to be a participant in. And that is the power of intention. In order to tap into this power, we need to learn and embrace four specific steps as outlined by Wayne Dyer in his book about the subject of manifesting our intention. What he eloquently describes is that we first need to know this body that we reside within. It needs to be what we are tuned into, for it is our vehicle for connecting with the world and with the many others in it.

If we are not clear about our own body, if we are out of sync with it, if we are ill and out of good working condition, we are very distracted by our own self and that state of dis-ease to the point of having a restricted ability to connect with the world and with others. This makes sense, right? Because when we are ill in any manner, we generally want to isolate and incubate until we feel better or we want to have another by our side to tend to what we need because we cannot. In either case, it thwarts our energy.

The second step is that we need to then be in tune with our own internal wisdom, and we each have it. It is our strength within to tap into and to acknowledge and attend to in meaningful ways, and not tune away from. You know what it means to listen to your gut. We talk about gut reactions. We always talk about how we dismiss them. When we are patient, when we are open, we become harmonious with the self and allow wisdom to be present, and we learn here to balance the activity of our head and our heart. We become reasonable and wise as a result. We each know how sickening it feels when we are out of whack by being over-emotional, out of control, or so involved in our thinking-mind that we've forgotten how to feel anything at all, and we become dead to our senses.

Perhaps the most essential part of this formula of steps is that of love. Love is the core. It is the part of life that gives it meaning. We cannot deny the power that love has, and the only people I have ever encountered who try to deny it are those who were deeply injured by being in love. In this case, love is about being in love with life and what you are doing with your time here. When we love what we are doing and we love our self, everyone makes note of it; there is no way to fabricate it from nothing. It either is or is not, and the vibrance it produces is spectacular.

The fourth step is about assuming a position of relaxation. Some call it surrender. I invite you to hear my words here and decide what is most appealing to you because the head games here are important to pay close attention to. You need to understand the concepts and then select what the words are that help you to adopt and maintain what is necessary. The issue is that control is something most of us strive for, and it is an ever unattainable goal. The more we work and press to control anything aside from our own mind, the more we isolate ourselves from others. The more we meet with angst and despair, instead of aiming for control, we should relax with the notion that things will unfold and that everything that is supposed to be, will be. Whatever is there has some element we are invited to explore and in which to understand our opportunity.

Once you grasp this, it is so freeing. For me, I used to almost panic at the idea of forgoing control, but once I really looked, I then allowed myself to see. It made sense to me that I could find greater effectiveness in this mode for I could then be in some place of alignment, natural alignment, with whatever these invisible energies of the world are and intention took on a whole new meaning.

Across this series, I have only just opened doors to ideas and to exercises for you to try alongside introductions to ways of being and doing that are all designed to enrich you and your life experience. This episode is dedicated to continuing that by inviting you to look into your self deeply and ask what it is that you want. What is it that you desire from this life experience? What would you like to see happen?

Your Self Talk Script

I invite you to sit here now and envision what your life is without restriction, with a body you are tuned into, with a mind that is sharp and clear, and with an internal voice that allows you to experience your beautiful inner wisdom, a wisdom that is ancient and guided. I invite you to feel how in love you are with your life and your work. Imagine the ways that you let everyone around you know about your love affair with life and also with them. Make it beauty-filled and safe and clear and clean and happy. Envision that love empowering you to win at everything you do where wining means loving it, and knowing every outcome is what it is supposed to be, and the opportunities are rich for you to explore. Take all of that in, and be so deeply committed to it, and centered on it, knowing that it is not up to you alone to create your life. For you are not alone. None of us are. We are co-creators of this experience, with one another and with the universal source that brought us here . . . whatever that is.

Breathe, rest, relax, envision, be of wellness in this moment. Know that you are managing your stress, your mind, and your life experience.

When you see me in the next episode, I will be sharing with you the reasons why stress managed is a life well lived and essentially pulling together the journey we've taken thus far and offering up more for you to assimilate and contemplate for accessing the strength within you.

To view the video: www.drdebcarlin.com

SELF-ASSESSMENT
Expectation of Success

Prospecting is an old art, a practice. In today's culture, it has many con-notations—some positive and some negative. In our context, it is about a dimension of intentionality. When we prospect, we are looking for who might be a person or thing to help us to succeed at what we are trying to achieve. It is the act of observation and judgment to find the likely customer. Customers are important to us in both parts of our lives: the business and the personal. We prospect for clients, customers, friends, lovers, spouses, advocates—for everything.

What is the process that you engage in to prospect?

What's your track record, do you know?

The opening question for you here is: how well do you prospect? Think carefully, reply to the questions.

Answer honestly. If you don't, then this is just a silly game that is a waste of time, especially yours.

1 = not at all   9 = all the way

1. I have a daily mindset of prospecting.

   1   2   3   4   5   6   7   8   9

2. I think of prospects only as potential customers for my business.

   1   2   3   4   5   6   7   8   9

3. I am very good at identifying somebody or something with potential.

   1   2   3   4   5   6   7   8   9

4. I have a definitive system for prospecting.

   1   2   3   4   5   6   7   8   9

5. I have prospected successfully in my business life.

   1   2   3   4   5   6   7   8   9

6. I have prospected successfully in my personal life.

   1   2   3   4   5   6   7   8   9

7. I can say with confidence that I have high expectations for success for myself.

   1   2   3   4   5   6   7   8   9

8. I am confident the people in my work life would agree with my assessment.

   1   2   3   4   5   6   7   8   9

9. I am confident that the people in my personal life would agree with my assessment.

   1   2   3   4   5   6   7   8   9

PLAN OF ACTION TOOL
Expectations of Success

Tony Robbins wrote the book *Awaken the Giant Within* back in 1991 when he was referring to himself as Anthony Robbins. He has sold millions of copies of the book and has given his presentation about the subject to hundreds of millions of people all over the globe. Amazing.

Equally as amazing is his skill at prospecting.

To Tony, everyone is a someone and no one is a nobody. He sees potential in every person and all things. His pitch is that we need to take immediate control of our mental, emotional, physical, and financial destiny—right now. Prior to writing about the inner giant, he wrote about the **Unlimited Power** he sees existing in every human being.

I've had the amazing pleasure of not only meeting this awesome creature, but spending time with him and interacting with him. He is what he writes and speaks. My affinity towards this man is his genuine reality and his absolute clear vision that he is on this planet to help people wake up and be alive. I'm right there with him in this line of thinking. And prospecting is all about seeing an opportunity, a way to have something of benefit happen. When you are in business, you need to find opportunities to make things happen . . . whatever those things are.

Following is the Action Plan to help you achieve this.

Step 1

Obtain a copy of each book below and study them intently:

Awaken The Giant Within

Unlimited Power

The Imposter Phenomenon

Dr. Pauline Rose Clance wrote the phenomenal book listed above that has been a best seller in the academic world, *The Imposter Phenomenon: Overcoming the Fear That Haunts Your Success.* Written in 1985, she captures the inner dialogue we all fall prey to at one moment or another as we suffer our fears of failure and allow the prospects to get away because we have some glimmer of self-doubt. Her work facilitates us all putting guilt in a back pocket and allowing our promise to shine through.

Step 2

Adopt the following:

"The belief that becomes truth for me . . . is that which allows me the best use of my strength, the best means of putting my virtues into action."—ANDRÉ GIDE

He was a cad of sorts and had a rather tortured life. However, perhaps it was through his own agony that he wrote and inspired other great writers and came to be aware that in order to achieve, you must believe, and you must create a surge of energy inside of your own self in order to step out and accomplish.

Questions to answer:

What is your energetic voice inside of you telling you about your focus on success?

How do you define success for yourself?

What actions are you willing to put into place to create a view of open opportunity where prospecting becomes viable?

As you ask yourself these questions, does anything happen to you physically?

The association between your thoughts and your physiological response cements the thinking and will either propel you into action or keep you from it. What are you willing to do to awaken the giant inside of you and allow yourself to feel your right to enormous success . . . success at every level in your life?

List 5 thoughts and 5 physical reactions and make a commitment to them here:

1.

2.

3.

4.

5.

SELF-ASSESSMENT
Movement & Desire

You've been moving in this event with the guidance of a world-class expert. You completed an opening self-assessment about your ability; now you need to tune into your desire.

Remember the vision of the little baby who can move and stretch and bend and enjoy taking flexibility for granted. You've gotten some new exposure to movement with us.

Has it shifted your desires?

Opened your desires?

The opening question for you here is:

Is it important for you to move freely throughout your life span? Think carefully, and reply to the questions.

Answer honestly. If you don't, then this is just a silly game that is a waste of time , especially yours.

1 = not at all   9 = all the way

1. I have an extremely flexible body and this is important to me.

1   2   3   4   5   6   7   8   9

2. I am able to move my body without restriction or pain anywhere and this is important to me.

1   2   3   4   5   6   7   8   9

3. I am completely functional, no awkwardness or stiffness in any part of my body.

1   2   3   4   5   6   7   8   9

4. I can move my arms with full range of movement and this is important to me.

1   2   3   4   5   6   7   8   9

5. I can move my hips with full range of movement and this is important to me.

1   2   3   4   5   6   7   8   9

6. I can move my legs with full range of movement and zero pain in my knees.

1   2   3   4   5   6   7   8   9

7. I can move and walk and my feet are comfortable, no pain, no aches, no problem.

1   2   3   4   5   6   7   8   9

8. I am desirous of being able to move like a Pilates expert, flexible and pain free.

1   2   3   4   5   6   7   8   9

9. I am confident that the people in my personal life would agree with my assessment.

1   2   3   4   5   6   7   8   9

PLAN OF ACTION TOOL
Expectations of Success

Look at the answers you provided on the previous page.

Is this important to you?

You decide and make a written statement for each one of the following about what you are ready and willing to do.

Take a class

Hire an expert for personal work

Commit to a schedule daily

Outline your goals here and map out the plan so you know what is right for you:

Stress Managed Is a Life Well Lived

How can we ever hope to live well if our world is on a state of constant angst and stress and strain ? And does it ever stop? Do things calm down? Does the news in the media ever get positive? How do we hope to live a life where our stress is managed?

By now, you have a clear picture that it happens when you allow yourself to train your mind and then take specific steps to find your heart, your life purpose, your love, your loves, what brings forth passion for you, and what prompts your creative side in ways that delight you.

Do you now look at other people who are running frantically around and buzzing about their busy-ness factor and their many crazy problems and see that they are invested in each aspect of it all? I hope I forever retain my compassion for my fellow human beings, but I also want to see clearly how nutty we can become if we don't pay attention to what we are doing each moment.

I had a business partner who would always inject into conversations how busy he is. He would say I have fifty me-mails to answer, I have twenty-three people wanting to see me and get my advice, I have a voice message center that is full. I have so much to do . . . I am so busy. And this usually came at a time when he knew there was a request en-route for some kind of help. I finally got tired of this game and boldly asked: Does it ever occur to you that I actually have a busy schedule, that I have many e-mails and phone calls and appointments? I just don't talk about it. I don't mention it.

He didn't reply, and I continued with, "It is a fact that we each get seven days each week and each day has twenty-four hours, and we are in charge of what we do with that time. As far as how we allocate our energies across that time, we decide how to book it or release it, but when one person proclaims how tied up he or she is, instead of sounding admirably important, it sounds arrogant and actually stupid. It's like you have forgotten to pay attention to getting some time to breathe and to rest. Even world leaders schedule that time into their planners.

The conversation ended with no further rebuttals of how busy and important he was, but I observe this man and the degree to which he is stressed. He bites at people. He is curt, and rude, and he's actually cruel at times, really thoughtless. I worry for him because it eventually all catches up with you, eventually. In fact, we are no longer business partners because I became so aware of this counterproductive behavior and the impact it had on me and on the people we worked with, I decided I could not afford to be a part of that kind of orbit. It infects everything I am intentional about. I am not surprised to hear about major cardiac problems people experience with this kind of stress.

You've heard about the language of the heart and when you embrace that knowledge it comes to take on a kind element in your world, one where you feel the impact of the thoughts you have, emotions you feel, and words you employ to express your *self* and you release your *self* from a state of dis ease. It is so simple and so basic, but it takes a lifetime to arrive at a place where we can begin to hear it, learn it, know it, and want it. I hope you're here.

The whole idea of this series and the notion of the strength within you is about coming to a place of being your own best—and you fill in the blank here—but know this: we each need to find how to be at our best. I am so aware that I am a work in progress. I have so much I love doing, so much I am clearly intentional about. I love that. I hope that each dream I have is on target but I know somewhere inside of me that if it is not, there is another one that will come into my view and invite me to explore it. And that will be a good thing.

I wish for you a life that is not sick, not harried, and not uncomfortable, but is a life that is full of beauty and love and intelligence and passion, with a balance for the head and heart and with deep faith and intention for every bit of that strength within you to be realized. This is it, this experience. My vote is that we enjoy it. I hope you have loved this series and that you want more for yourself, much more. You deserve it.

Your Self Talk Script

Sit here now. See it all before your eyes, your mind's eyes. Breathe with contentment, a contentment that you have never before known like you do now. Embrace it. Become intentional about it. See it. Feel it. Think it. Love it. Keep it here and continue to breathe and enjoy this time, it is yours. It is all about the strength within you.

To view the video: www.drdebcarlin.com

HOLMES & RAHE SCALE OF STRESS

In 1967 psychiatrists Thomas Holmes and Richard Rahe examined the medical records of over 5,000 medical patients as a way to determine whether stressful events might cause illnesses. Patients were asked to tally a list of forty-three life events based on a relative score. A positive correlation of 0.118 was found between their life events and their illnesses.

Their results were published as the Social Readjustment Rating Scale (SRRS), known more commonly as the **Holmes and Rahe Stress Scale**. Subsequent validation has supported the links between stress and illness.

Rahe carried out a study in 1970 testing the reliability of the stress scale as a predictor of illness. The scale was given to 2,500 US sailors and they were asked to rate scores of "life events" over the previous six months. Over the next six months, detailed records were kept of the sailors' health. There was a +0.118 correlation between stress scale scores and illness, which was sufficient to support the hypothesis of a link between life events and illness.

In conjunction with the Cornell medical index assessing, the stress scale correlated with visits to medical dispensaries, and the H&R stress scale's scores also correlated independently with individuals dropping out of stressful underwater demolitions training due to medical problems. The scale was also assessed against different populations within the United States.

To measure stress according to the Holmes and Rahe Stress Scale, the number of "Life Change Units" that apply to events in the past year of an individual's life are added and the final score will give a rough estimate of how stress affects health.

LIFE EVENT	LIFE CHANGE UNITS
Death of a spouse	100
Divorce	73
Marital separation	65
Imprisonment	63
Death of a close family member	63
Personal injury or illness	53
Marriage	50
Dismissal from work	47
Marital reconciliation	45
Retirement	45
Change in health of family member	44
Pregnancy	40
Business readjustment	39
Gain a new family member	39
Sexual difficulties	39
Change in financial state	38
Death of a close friend	37
Change to different line of work	36
Change in frequency of arguments	35
Major mortgage	32
Foreclosure of mortgage or loan	30
Change in responsibilities at work	29

Life Event	Life Change Units
Child leaving home	29
Trouble with in-laws	29
Outstanding personal achievement	28
Spouse starts or stops work	26
Begin or end school	26
Change in living conditions	25
Revision of personal habits	24
Trouble with boss	23
Change in residence	20
Change in working hours or conditions	20
Change in schools	20
Change in recreation	19
Change in church activities	19
Change in social activities	18
Minor mortgage or loan	17
Change in sleeping habits	16
Change in number of family reunions	15
Change in eating habits	15
Vacation	13
Christmas	12
Minor violation of law	11

Score of 300+ At risk of illness.
Score of 150–299+ Risk of illness is moderate (reduced by 30% from the above risk).
Score 150– Only have a slight risk of illness.

PLAN OF ACTION TOOL
Creating a Plan of Wellness

The most important thing to do with information is to use it wisely. Regardless of where you landed in the scores for the stress index, the goal is to have you determine how best to manage it and fold a plan of action into your Blueprint.

Life is indeed filled with stress—it is a natural component of our experience. There are costs associated with everything we do, fun or otherwise; stress is a byproduct. Let's not let it impair us as we build a Blueprint for a Successfully Integrated Life.

We can turn to www.drdebcarlin.com for a more expanded understanding of what stress is and how we can manage it effectively. Once we grasp and own these concepts, we can begin to get a quiet focus on the plan of intention for our life.

What is stress?

UNDERSTANDING WHAT STRESS IS

People most often inquire as to the *effects of stress*, but the opening question really needs to be: What is stress? This is important because it is experienced by people in a wide variety of ways, and what is stressful to one is often not to another.

In its most basic form, stress is the result of something being impinged upon. That something, when it is a person, can experience the impingement as being either physical or emotional, and sometimes both. Impingement is, of course, some form of a pinch or an intrusion or an unwelcome something. When it is physical, it is anything from extreme temperatures to whatever causes physical pain or discomfort. When it is emotional, the same is true but in a very different sense.

What follows is a definition from Encarta Dictionary:

Impinge

1. Interfere
   To affect the limits of something, especially a right or law, often causing some kind of restriction
   e.g., Members claimed that canceling the ballot impinged on their voting rights

2. Strike
   To strike or hit something
   e.g., A loud noise can impinge on the eardrum, causing temporary hearing damage

To some people, loud music is very stressful because of the manner in which it hits their ear and they find there is no way to escape the attack of sound. That form of strike is stressful to the body. There are, of course, people who hear that same loudness and sit in it with apparent enjoyment.

Are you curious about the difference?

Let's take another example and look a bit more closely.

For some, the physical temperature of 65 degrees feels perfect and to others, it is too cool. The same can be said of temperatures in the 90s or the teens. Our experience of the physical temperature depends upon our attire, the exact situation, our state of physical health, and our mental well-being.

With respect to emotional impingement, it is experienced when something happens that meets with our disapproval at some level. It can be like the example of the ballots being canceled, an event that would leave members feeling unvalued and without a mechanism for being productively expressive. It is easy to imagine that this kind of experience would promote frustration. Frustration is stressful; no one enjoys it.

Physical and emotional stresses are often kept in separate categories, but in my work as well as in my personal life, I have made special note that they are nearly always tied together. Our experience of everything physically is closely related and is intricately integrated into our emotional experience of it.

For example, I'm from Chicago and I have a lifetime of happy memories of playing in the ice and snow and loving every portion of it. I was with friends and family that I enjoyed. For me, the blustery winter means fun and laughter and with the time out in the cold being followed with just as much fun when it was time to head indoors for seats around a fireplace while sipping on hot chocolate and snuggling with loved ones. I pair the experience of cold with the experience of the warmth that follows, and it all becomes pleasant, not stressful. I also associate it with being bundled up in warm wool socks that were hand knitted by my mother, as were my scarves and hats and mittens. I also had leggings and tights and sweaters and snowsuits that kept me bundled and protected from the wet and cold.

However, for someone who grew up with a shortage of heat in the house and only light clothing to wear and perhaps not enough warm food, the cold will elicit memories quite different from mine. Cold for them will most likely mean deprivation, and therefore feel very frustrating and stressful.

The core issue here is that the associations we make between a physical sort of experience and our mental interpretation leads to a strong connection. The trick, when it comes to understanding stress, is to recognize how it is both a matter of how it is presented to us and then also is a matter of how we allow our mind to perceive it and re-interpret it.

Managing stress is a matter of mind games. Our mind loves, and craves, games.

EFFECTS OF STRESS

Each of us has an intuitive sense of how stress effects a person. Every human has had the direct experience of stress, both physically and emotionally.

Once upon a time, when I was in college, I did an internship in a biology laboratory. The research being conducted was cellular. We studied one-cell creatures and their response to copper. My job entailed poking them with a copper probe while they resided in their lab dishes. It was a strange experience because with a one-cell structure, there wasn't much to see. However, what I did notice was the recoil action that was consistent. After time and again of these poking, there was death, and even though the work was done under microscope because of the size of these creatures, it was uncomfortable. Why? I hope it is obvious to you as the reader here that even with such a distinctly different form of life, I knew intuitively that I was imposing a form of stress upon the object. It caused me to feel intrusive. Needless to say, this was not a career path I pursued.

Stress for us as humans is not a whole lot different. When we are poked by the dentist, by a bully, or by a tree branch, we can only tolerate it for a short time before it becomes unbearable. There are forms of torture that entail only innocent drops of water being continuously administered. But one drop at a time over and over again dripping to the same place on your forehead is annoying and guaranteed to produce a stressful reaction.

What is a stress reaction?

I predict that there will always be argument about what happens first, whether the mind reacts first or the body is the first to react. But from my perspective the two are so closely aligned, it becomes a moot point. What is important is to pay close attention to what can be done to handle whatever comes towards you that elicits the awareness that stress is present.

There is the classic explanation of the fight or flight syndrome first written about by Walter Bradford Cannon, MD. (October 19, 1871– October 1, 1945) an American physiologist, professor, and chairman of the Department of Physiology at Harvard Medical School. He coined the term "fight or flight response," and he expanded on Claude Bernard's concept of homeostasis. He popularized his theories in his book *The Wisdom of the Body*, first published in 1932. His theory states that animals react to threats with a general discharge of the sympathetic nervous system, priming the animal for fighting or fleeing. This response was later recognized as the first stage of a general adaptation syndrome (later written about by Hans Selye) that regulates stress responses among vertebrates and other organisms. (See http://en.wikipedia.org/wiki/Fight-or-flight_response, accessed 2012).

Although it seems a bit complex when first reviewing the information, it is actually quite simple to understand what takes place as a result of something either being actually stressful or being interpreted as stressful. We get ready for action.

Catecholamine hormones facilitate immediate physical reactions associated with a preparation for violent muscular action. These include the following, which are classic:

* Acceleration of heart and lung action

* Paling or flushing, or alternating between both

* Inhibition of stomach and upper-intestinal action to the point where digestion slows down or stops

* General effect on the sphincters of the body
* Constriction of blood vessels in many parts of the body
* Liberation of nutrients (particularly fat and glucose) for muscular action
* Dilation of blood vessels for muscles
* Inhibition of the lacrimal gland (responsible for tear production) and salivation
* Dilation of pupil (mydriasis)
* Relaxation of bladder
* Inhibition of erection
* Auditory exclusion (loss of hearing)
* Tunnel vision (loss of peripheral vision)
* Acceleration of instantaneous reflexes
* Shaking

The idea of relaxation brings forth all sorts of reactions from people, especially when I recommend it as a specific practice to learn for wellness. More often than not, people tell me that they know how to relax and do it pretty well.

However, as Americans, we actually don't do the relaxation part very well at all, although we do the have-fun part very well. There is a difference. I rely upon my instruments of a blood pressure cuff and the second hand on my watch to provide biofeedback for people in order to make my points about the benefits of relaxation clear and also make clear how they differ from basic fun.

There is nothing wrong with fun. I prescribe that we each engage in it daily. However, the mind and the body need true release from stress and activity daily if we are to experience and enjoy true well-being.

When I teach the Relaxation Response, which is a very simple routine, people witness their heart rate slow down and become regulated, and they also see their blood pressure drop to a safe, healthy level. This is important because our organs need time to be attended to in ways that assist in their recovery from how active we are and how much we overtax them daily. Americans get sick and die from diseases that relate to organ illness, so we need to take effective care of these invisible parts of our body.

The practice of meditation is known around the world and comes in many forms. There are religious formats as well as secular. You can practice in silence or with music or sounds of nature. The goal is to provide yourself a physical space that allows you to release from this world and go into your head and feel free and relaxed inside of your own self, for the benefit of your mind and body.

Chanting monks engage in chanting because it readies them for a deeper experience of prayerfulness.

Yogis emit a mantra to align their mind and body with one another and ready them for meditation and movement that relaxes and refreshes.

We can each adopt a relaxation pose and experience that brings us calm and allows us to realize a deeper relationship not only to the self but to a higher power, one that gives our existence greater meaning beyond our own daily experience.

This embracing of a higher power, whatever you label it, is repeatedly shown to add value, wellness, and longevity to human life. It is often thought that sleep produces a state of relaxation. But from sleep research it has been discovered that what we avoid thinking about during the day, we dream about during the night, and it is not always relaxing. In fact, sleep disorders are prevalent in America, increasingly more each year.

Two factors related to sleep

1. When sleeping we are often grinding our teeth as a result of tension, releasing gastric juices into the gut for the reason, or experiencing dreams that are disturbing either consciously or unconsciously.

2. Even when we intend on sleep, we don't often get enough of it or a restful experience of it given the 24/7 nature of our world culture. During the daylight hours, when we are at our best, we can learn the simple exercises of relaxation for the mind and body. Practice them to not only experience relaxation during the day, but have an enhanced sleep at night. It is a win-win scenario.

THE PLAN OF INTENTION FOR OUR LIFE

Look again at the scores you tallied on the Holmes & Rahe instrument. Decide what it is that you are done with and can move on from—healthfully.

Be honest about what you're in the middle of and acknowledge the ways in which it causes angst; once you own it, you can tend to it. List three positive things you can do to take care of yourself in the stressful scenario:

1.

2.

3.

and insert when you'll actually do them.

Do the same for the stresses you know are upcoming.

Arrange your life to offset the negative impact of stress that is unavoidable. Add positives.

"The beginning of anxiety
is the end of faith,
and the beginning of faith
is the end of anxiety..."

—GEORGE MUELLER

Section V

THE BIG PICTURE WITH DETAILS

Blueprint for a Successfully Intentional & Integrated Life

Reexamining the Assessments

Understanding Your Story

A Portrait of You

Blueprint for a Successfully Intentional & Integrated Life

The structure is nearly complete. You're about ready to move in. The officials have nearly signed off with their approvals. Each of the furnishings you've ordered alongside every detail of interior trim and exterior landscaping is sketched onto the Blueprint in your mind, but you have to place it onto the paper to ensure it actually happens.

The structure you've been building is the only place you are ever going to reside. It is yours. You own it—100%.

The stakes are high because you've invested every beat of your heart, every year of your life, every thought and emotion into this dwelling. It simply has to be terrific, comfortable, safe, and smart. You are dedicated to ensuring it.

Before you go any further, you need to check the overall design . . .

Look at your Blueprint and transcribe any responses not already there.

Look at it quietly . . .

You need to know every inch of it.

Insert your replies onto each square of the assessments while being careful to color code your responses as indicated on the legend.

Think about any shifts that have occurred and any you'd like to have happen.

Look at the deck of cards that are available to you and review what they say. They contain the verbiage from each assessment to refresh your memory and get you thinking.

As you sit there with your plan in front of you, consider what you are willing to do in the way of making a deal with your *self* to get to where you are eager to be in this life.

If you commit to what you want on each line of the deal square, you'll have a plan of action reminder right there. You can visit it, change it, keep the hard copy version, and add the digital component however you'd like to.

The idea is to just do it. Do it now. Visit often to make upgrades, renovate, and rearrange the furnishings—this is where you live!

Reexamining the Assessments

The best use of a test is the re-test. Now is the time to retake the assessment you did earlier. Retake it and then use this open space to write your thoughts with respect to any shifts, ideas, frustrations, motivations, and inspirations.

The ones you've got left to retake are as follows:
  The Faith Factor
  Expectations of Success
  Movement & Desire

Take a good look at the assessments. You've worked your way across them. The time has come for you to open your Blueprint for a Successfully Intentional and Integrated Life and begin to enter the numbers. This exercise is going to give a full perspective about where you are in your mind and in your body and your heart. You'll see where you want to maneuver things for your ultimate benefit.

"You can tell if someone is clever by their answers, and you can tell if they are wise by their questions."

Understanding Your Story

Take a few moments, right now.

Remember where you were before you picked up this document with respect to the feelings you had, based on the thoughts you had, about what the story of your life was. Recall everything you had in your mind and in your heart about the why—why you are the way you are and why your life is the way it is.

Give yourself a moment and ask yourself if you now have a little bit different perception of who you are and why your life is the way that it is, in part, because of the way in which you've allowed the story to be written . . . to date.

Do you now understand that you have some authority, power, influence, and ability to shift gears and rewrite the story—because you do indeed have control—over your mind.

Rewrite your story here, with the power of intention, knowing that you want to create your best life yet. Utilize every tool within this document over and again, use every link provided, take us up on the offer to participate where we extend invitations, and just make it happen.

It's all about you . . . just do it.

A Portrait of You & Your Life

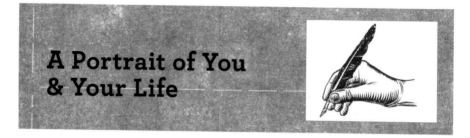

The self-portrait is perhaps the most beautiful creation you will ever put your hand and heart to make it happen . . . lovingly towards your *self* . . .

ACKNOWLEDGMENTS

There is no project that gets done in this life as a solo effort. There are always people to thank, to express sincere gratitude towards for what their contribution has been and what it has meant. I'm so appreciative of the people in my life, the ones who gave me my life and the ones I have collected as a result of the goodness of the power of intention and all the prayers within those lifelong intentions. My gratitude is for far more than just the pages here because these are merely a representation of a program, a message, a full mission, and that mission is one that I now recognize as being what I've been called to do for my entire life. It is about service, about being of service to others. Every blessing we receive is bestowed upon us for a reason. In my case, I choose to view the reasons as an invitation to do more—more with my skills and more with my life, however possible. It seems the blessings I have received have been abundant.

My parents, **Warren & Lorretta Carlin** . . . now the dearly departed, continue to be a central influence and inspiration for me with every breath . . . they were magnificent in their own life and they are angelic guides for me in mine. I am forever grateful.

My family of origins and my extended family are certainly acknowledged here as well—so many lessons learned, so many opportunities to expand my abilities and open my heart to learn discipline, aim to become exquisite with patience, to persevere to know humility, and crave wisdom. I am appreciative of every moment experienced.

To **Tara Rose Gladstone**, whose interview of me for a piece she was developing about peace, love, and healing led to an immediate connection. Not only did she introduce me to her dad, but that introduction led to a fascinating opportunity and a relationship that is very significant to me. Tara, you are a joy in my life, a gift to my heart, an inspiration across the week, and a most valued asset to my work. Thank you for so many different gifts you bring into my world.

To my literary agent, for whom I have prayed to obtain when the heavens deemed it right, the renowned **William Gladstone**. From the opening conversation, there was a gentle connection that resulted in a contractual agreement that has launched my spirit and hopefully my writing career in ways that align with the abundance of the universe. I am grateful that such a power-filled human being would avert their attention in my direction and open doors of opportunity. I pray to be worthy of the investment.

To my publisher, **Kenzi Sugihara**, the man with the softest voice and most gentle commanding ways—when our mutual Mr. Gladstone made this all possible, I knew it would be fabulous. However, getting to work with you, **Kenichi Sugihara**, and then **Nancy Sugihara**, I knew the energy was something truly magnificent and blessed. What could I possibly say in the manner of a thank you that would express my gratitude for everything you have invested in me and in my work? It is my intention to make you proud to put your name with mine to make good works happen.

Especially to **Nancy Sugihara**, my editor at SelectBooks, I should hire a sky writing airplane to script a message over Manhattan that includes a large thank you! Whenever I have read the gratitude that an author has written to their editor, I have felt a certain yearning to have that process in place, inside a great relationship. Sharing the responsibility of getting this book into shape with you, kind and lovely you, has been another prayer answered for me. This has been a great experience and I am forever grateful for your guidance, leadership, attitude, heart, and skillful mind.

The team I have collected for Partners In Excellence LLC is nothing short of exquisite; each is an entrepreneur with dreams they are pursuing. I appreciate the time I have with people for whatever the duration.

Jamison Sweet, once my engineer on The K Factor, and also the Director and Co-Producer of *The Series 16*, which gave rise to this book and the event series associated with it. You've been a friend, consistent help, and loving inspiration on this project since its inception. Thank you.

Steve Smart, who is a talented consultant, eager to be a source of reliable help and tangible benefit. Steve is what his name bears—smart, and then he is more. He is a great person, and genuine inspiration.

Cody Long, who spent many hours on the details of the first version of this book at the computer, contributing creative ideas as she listened to mine, talking with our printing vendor, meeting with the artists, and with many people whose help we've needed to enlist for one aspect of this ordeal known as a project, I thank you. For providing a fabulous country outlet for my mind to release into nature and enjoy the scene in Labadie, Missouri and for your friendship, initiative, thoughtfulness, loyalty, and diligence—I thank you.

Dan Neves, who is a talented sound mixer and was the audio man for *The Series 16*, thank you for your unending support and friendship over the course this entire endeavor—you're awesome.

For my additional assistants who keep me organized and on track with every detail of ever growing activity as our company expands along with our message for the world—thank you.

Bryan Haynes, whose works of art I immediately fell madly in love with the first time I saw them, came to me through Cody. He heard the story of the work herein and of the vision of what we needed; he created his rendition of Atlas, now an important component of our brand. Atlas transitions from overwhelmed to managing life well. He also re-created the classic Thinker for me by adding the heart we need. The toolbox alongside our soup can icons come from his genius. Thank you, Bryan, so much, you are a brilliant talent. www.artbybryanhaynes.com

Peggy Lents, of Lents & Associates, who has become an important guide in my life, a very endeared friend, and a creative public relations strategist. Taking me on as a new challenge, I came to you loaded with ideas and you pushed me to better articulate and become tangible about each one of them. I adore what you do and how you make things happen, Peggy. Together, with your team, my name and brand will become more recognizable and we will have powerful opportunity to extend our services further and more deeply. I thank you for your investment in me expressed through your loving enthusiasm, and strong pushes. You are smart, witty, intuitive, and wonderful.

Ellen Sherberg, Publisher of the St Louis Business Journal (SLBJ), allowed me to capture a moment of her time, share my vision, and gain her support—an invaluable person to know and strive to impress. Ellen, you are a powerful leader, it is a privilege to have you in my life, you inspire me. Thank you.

And from Ellen, comes **Jennifer Tompras** who I met at the SLBJ . . . a bright sparkle of energy, love, support, and unending enthusiasm for what all of this is about—I thank you over and again because you rekindle my enthusiasm with yours.

My domestic staff, each of whom keep my home life lovely by tending to all the tasks I simply choose not to have time for—you make everything possible with the hours you free up for my energy to be invested elsewhere, like in these pages. You each add the elements to this home front that give it the ambiance, the feel, the security necessary for this to be my sanctuary. **Chris and Peter Napoli, Gregg Hamann, Dawn Lebcowitz**—I thank you each for your work, which is tireless and keeps me energized.

To two of my associates within Partners In Excellence LLC whom I have invited to come share the platform with me to deliver the messaging of an intentional life where we build upon our inner strength to be healthy, happy, and productive—Mark Levy and Larry Shapiro.

Mark Levy, you are my dear friend and Chicago internist and you are a phenomenon in my life. The work you did with my mother and me, and that we have done since her passing into heaven, has motivated me to believe more fully that this messaging is essential; you see this as a physician and reinforce the ideas that we share about how intentional we need to have our life be. I thank you for every bit of your friendship. You are nothing short of fabulous.

Larry Shapiro, for your patience and friendship as this project unfolds. You are a great addition to the team—generous, bright, very futuristic in your thinking, and 100% genteel. Thank you.

For **Charlotte Miller**, my friend for more than thirty years, who died during the course of this project—. sadly, valiantly, and far too young. A bright spirit in the world, an incredible mind, with fortitude and inner strength that was notable and memorable, I made a promise to her that her name and her story would live on through me and through this work—it shall, lovingly. I thank you for decades of deep to deep connection. Our friendship was genuine and unforgettable. I will miss you, always.

To my lifelong friend, originally **Juanita Deterding**, now happily married and known as **Juanita Vanderpoel with her husband, Al**. You two are a pair of my favorites. You are always so good to me, lovingly encouraging my message and providing ideas for how I can improve what I do and how I do it. I love you and thank you for every moment of your investment in all of this.

To my darling, **Jim Baumgartner, and his beautiful wife, Pippa**, I extend gratitude, love, and deep appreciation. You are supportive of me in ways that make a powerful difference in my abilities—thank you, forever.

My cousin, **Tom Kay and his wife Angela**, whose love and ongoing support and encouragement mean the world to me in a thousand different ways—I love you dearly. I thank you for always being ready to offer your guidance and wisdom, it is always perfect timing.

To **Monsignor Sudekum**, who saved my life at a time when I questioned my worth and who inspired me to be everything possible as a way to honor my parents . . . you are a spiritual guide, mentor, and a dear friend to me and I am forever grateful. Together with **Monsignor Deitz**, you two men have been a truly awesome part of my life and a very important component of my work. I love you and thank you both.

To my exquisite consultants from the **Tony Robbins** organization, **Bill Baker** and **Brook Bishop**, you two are a life force, a bright and guiding energy, a smart resource, tough critics, and 100 percent on target daily. Tony Robbins has a magic touch that you each exude: you know I adore Tony and what his life work is all about. I love that he has both of you on his team so that I can also have you on mine. I am forever thankful for our relationships and the work we do—wow! Fiji awaits us over and again.

To the authors whose works have been featured within, so much gratitude lives within my heart and mind for you . . . thank you for your words and works.

To my new partners, **Wellbridge Athletic Club & Spa** in Clayton Missouri, who are marvelously investing in this entire program by offering our audience very special access to their facility, this is enormous; together we will have a fabulous opportunity to healthfully influence many lives. Thank you General Manager **Greg McCarthy**.

To my dear friend, **Russ Abell** who served as General Manager at the **Hilton Orrington** in Evanston Illinois for more than two decades and is my dear friend. I thank you for your belief in what this project and overall mission means and what it can do for our audiences. Your enthusiasm has been impactful.

And to **Brenda and Rick** of **B & J Printing** in Washington, Missouri . . . thank you for making this possible. Without you, my little Canon Pixma would be mighty tired.

And to each and every person I have ever encountered, whether we acknowledge it or not, conscious or unconscious, we all have an impact upon one another and it is meaningful. We need one another for cooperation and for productivity that grows from that. My constant prayer and my intent is that this material . . . this book, and the programs that go alongside it are all beneficial to those who receive it.

ILLUSTRATION & PHOTO CREDITS

Drawings throughout the text were created by Bryan Haynes.

Photos are from the following sources:

page iv	image source istockphoto, © da-kuk
page 17	photo of Dr. Deb Carlin © Lee Steffen
page 32	image source istockphoto, © Grégory DUBUS
page 38	image source istockphoto, © ola_p
page 48	image source istockphoto, © amygdala_imagery
page 52	image source istockphoto, © 7000
page 89	image source istockphoto, © Anna Berkut
page 97	image source istockphoto, © Jeff Biglan
page 105	image source istockphoto, © red_moon_rise
page 111	image source istockphoto, © red_moon_rise
page 115	image source istockphoto, © ImagineGolf
page 134	image source istockphoto, © pixalot
page 145	image source istockphoto, © pixalot
page 151	image source istockphoto, © ImagesbyTrista
page 159	image source istockphoto, © photoGartner
page 169	image source istockphoto, © Jasmina007
page 192	image source iStockPhoto, © travellinglight
page 201	image source istockphoto, © 9comeback
page 206	image source istockphoto, © ImagineGolf
page 214	image source istockphoto, © Grégory DUBUS
page 220	image source istockphoto, © Rolphus
page 224	image source istockphoto, © Sezer66
page 233	image source istockphoto, © 7000
page 269	photo of Dr. Deb Carlin © Lee Steffen

Architectural background © istockphoto/ildogesto
Blueprint background © istockphoto/belterz
Hand & quill pen drawing © istockphoto/John Woodcock

Index

Imposter Phenomenon, The (Clance), 226
Improvement
    personal areas, 70, 164
    professional areas, 70, 164
In-breath (inhalation), 60
Industry/inferiority, contrast, 16–17
Infancy (first year), trust/mistrust
    (contrast), 14–15
Infants
    actions, 99
    flexibility, 112
Information
    basics, xiii
    gathering, 33
Inhalation (in-breath), 60
Initiative/guilt, contrast, 16
Inner chatter, core focus, 44
Inner clarity, 191
Inner goodness, belief, 40
Inner perceptions, representation, 68
Inner strength, 33–37
    emergence, 213
    power, xii
    self-talk script, 38–39
    tapping, 150
Insignificance, feeling, 94
Instantaneous reflexes, acceleration, 242
Integrity/despair, contrast, 19–20
Intelligence, perspective, 27
Intelligence quotient (IQ), 116
Intentional Life Blueprint, 9
Intention, misconceptions, 216
Internal wisdom, 218
Intimacy, 147–150
    emotional intimacy, impact, 198
    isolation, contrast, 18
    personal intimacy, impact, 198
Intuitive space, 148
Is It Worth Dying For? (Eliot), 37
Iyengar, B.K.S., 63

J

Jobs, expectations, 6
Jois, K. Pattabhi, 63
Journaling exercise, 98, 146, 215

K

King, Bruce, 57
Klipper, Miriam Z., 120, 207

Kobasa, Suzanne, 127
Kryzanowska, Romana, 57, 58
Kundalini Yoga, 63
    Lifestyle, implementation, 64

L

Ladder Barrel, 58
Language of the Heart, The (Lynch), 34,
    141
Late adulthood, integrity/despair
    (contrast), 19–20
Laughter, complexity, 35
Leaders, effectiveness, 182
Learning techniques, acquaintance, 23
Letdown, sense (absence), 189
Life
    advantages, 29
    affirmation, 198
    alignment, 113
    balance, 181
    considerations, 28–31
        self-talk script, 32
    desire, 87
    dreams, 29–30
    events, scores, 235–237
    experience, impact, 80
    fulfillment, 72
    harmony, 72
    intention, plan, 244
    journey, xiii
    living, expectation, 5
    mechanics, xi
    mystery, 217
    planning, absence, 5–6
    portrait, 83, 139, 193, 252
    psychology, xi
    recapture, 93
    saving, 84–88, 90–96
        self-talk script, 89, 97
    simplicity, 195
    stress, management, 231–232
    work, balance (continuation), 157–158
        self-talk script, 159
Life Change Units, 235–237
Life cycle
    intention, xiv, 216–219
        self-talk script, 220–221
    product, 210
    stages (Erikson), 13
Lifestyle, 106–110

ABOUT THE AUTHOR

DR. DEBORAH CARLIN has a firm grip on what she demands of herself and her company. A nationally renowned expert in the field of the human condition and self-development, psychologist Dr. Carlin has helped individuals and guided leaders and corporations to "become the best version of themselves."

She received her masters and doctoral degrees from Saint Louis University where she won numerous awards for leadership, good citizenship, and academic performance. As a social psychologist with strong clinical training at Washington University Medical Center, she is a popular speaker and writer and does consulting engagements that focus on the performance of people within an organization. Her specialty is in concentrating on people's attitudes and perceptions to help them gain clarity so their performances can be at their peak.

Dr. Carlin focuses on results and knows what needs to be done, making it happen with a diligent and down-to-earth approach that makes things seem simple in the face of massive complexities. She has used the adversity in her own life experience to fuel a passion for life and to inspire and guide others to do the same.

As a result she and her company are best known for their repeated success in turning negative situations into positive, productive ones. Many identify her work as enhancing corporate culture, improving community unity, and bettering communication within groups of all types and sizes. As she states,

"All of this helps with overall performance, which is what every client is concerned about."

Dr. Deb is host of the Internet radio show The K Factor. You can tune in and hear her interview people from around the globe on BlogTalkRadio. com. In 2012 she began writing a twice-monthly column that appears in the *St Louis Business Journal*, and is dedicated to introducing the business community to reliable strategies for healthy work/life integration for productivity and overall healthfulness.

She appears in several editions of *Who's Who* as word spreads about her activities in business, academic, and civic community circles. She consistently volunteers for various organizations, working behind the scenes as she donates her time quietly. Her goal, on every project, is to be a partner and help people achieve a level of measurable performance excellence.

A self-proclaimed foodie, she is a fabulous cook and baker. She knows her way around the kitchen anywhere, and hers is a kitchen often filled with friends and business associates—she claims it is the best place to make a deal happen. Passionate about her garden, every holiday, and making life festive, she is also passionate about swimming, sailing, and anything to do with the water. She recently resumed a daily yoga practice that she believes fortifies her every bit as much as an active prayer life to sustain her inner strength.

"Lord, make me a channel of Your peace;

Where there is injury, pardon;

Where there is doubt, faith;

Where there is despair, hope;

Grant that I may not so much seek

to be understood as to understand."

—SAINT FRANCIS OF ASSISI
(born Giovanni Francesco di Bernardonei)